WONDERS
OF GOD'S CREATION

Eric Lyons

Wonders of God's Creation
by Eric Lyons

ISBN: 978-1-60063-066-8
Library of Congress: 2012951012

Printed in China

Layout and Design by Rob Baker

All Scripture quotations are from The New King James Version of the Bible, unless otherwise specified. Copyright © 1982, Thomas Nelson, Inc., Publishers.

Dedication

To the Wetumpka church of Christ. It has been a genuine joy to work with you since 2007. I commend your desire to declare the many wonders of our God.

"O God, You have taught me from my youth; and to this day I declare Your wondrous works" (Psalm 71:17).

Apologetics Press, Inc.
230 Landmark Drive
Montgomery, Alabama 36117
U.S.A.

Table of Contents

Have You Considered...?

InTRODUCtiON

HAVE YOU EVER STOPPED TO

WATCH A BALD EAGLE SOAR THROUGH THE SKY ON A CLEAR DAY? HAVE YOU EVER GOTTEN CHILL BUMPS when hearing the lion at the local zoo let out a spine-tingling roar? Do you enjoy observing monkeys hang from branches with one arm as they scratch their underarms with the other, all the while making their amusing sounds? And what about the lightning bugs that glow on dark summer nights—have you ever wondered how little beetles can produce light? God's animal creations are wonders of His design. They entertain us, inspire us, and most important, they remind us of how awesome the Creator is.

WONDERS OF GOD'S Creation

ALTHOUGH ANIMALS ARE CERTAINLY NOT THE MAIN THEME OF SCRIPTURE (THAT HONOR BELONGS TO our Lord Jesus Christ), the Bible does have a lot to say about them. For example, eight of the first nine chapters of the Bible mention animals. You can read about their creation in Genesis 1-2. Satan, the snake, as well as animal skins are mentioned in Genesis 3. Moses wrote about Abel's sheep in chapter four, while including much about animals in the account of Noah and the Flood in Genesis 6-9. From locusts to lions to leviathan, the Bible talks about a lot of different animals.

Consider the climax of the book of Job, when God spoke to Job out of a whirlwind. Instead of informing Job of the exact reasons for his serious suffering, God spoke to him about His Creation. Beginning in Job 38:39 and continuing through chapters 39, 40, and 41, God described several different animals, including the lion, the hawk, the behemoth, and leviathan. Of all of the things God could have said to Job, He spent some

77 verses talking about a variety of **animals.** He chose to teach Job about His [God's] all-powerful, all-knowing, supreme nature by describing some of His magnificent animal creation.

The fact is, we can learn a lot about God, the Creator and Sustainer of life, by studying the many kinds of creatures He made on days five and six of Creation. The super shock absorber between the beak and skull of the woodpecker could not have just evolved by time and chance. The lightning bug's ability to mix the proper chemicals to light up its back end is not the result of mindless evolution. The amazing abilities of these and all other animals testify to an infinitely intelligent and powerful Creator.

Since the time of Job, Noah, and even as long ago as Adam, man has learned some wonderful things about God by studying His amazing creation. In fact, 2,000 years ago the apostle Paul wrote the following words to Christians living in Rome: "Since the creation of the world His [God's] invisible attributes are clearly seen, being understood [by man] **by the things that are made** [example: **animals**], even His eternal power and Godhead" (Romans 1:20).

The prophet Isaiah once wrote about being allowed to see a vision of the throne of God. In the Lord's presence were angelic beings crying out one to another, "Holy, holy, holy is the Lord of hosts" (Isaiah 6:3). What is the basis of this praise? What is one reason we should be driven to worship God? Isaiah revealed one of the pillars of God's praise in the very next line: "**The whole earth is full of His [God's] glory**" (6:3).

The beauty, splendor, and design of God's earthly animals should drive us closer to the Creator. These "fingerprints" of God should make us stand in awe of Him. They should drive us to our knees in worship to Him. And they should compel us to tell others about Him. "Stand still and consider the wondrous works of God" (Job 37:14). "[D]eclare **His glory** among the nations, **His wonders** among all peoples. For the Lord is great and greatly to be praised" (1 Chronicles 16:24-25; Psalm 96:3-4).

1
MaMMals

The Creator's Incredible CAMEL

CAMELS MAY LIVE IN SOME OF THE HOTTEST PLACES ON EARTH, BUT THEY ARE SOME OF THE COOLEST (AND COMICAL) CREATURES THAT GOD CREATED.

Just one look at their skinny legs, knobby knees, wide feet, humped back, long neck, stretched face, bushy eyebrows, and big, floppy lips, and you can't help but chuckle. Just be careful not to laugh at a camel too long: you might irritate him. And if you bother him too much, he might just bite, kick, or even "spit" at you. Well, it is not really saliva (which humans frequently spit). Camels actually burp up partly digested food called "cud" and spray their agitators by flinging the greenish gunk from their floppy lips. You may not have to worry about this with well-trained camels, but if you agitate a crabby camel, watch out!

ONE-HUMP WONDERS

Some camels have two humps. These camels are known as Bactrian [BACK-tree-un] camels and live mostly in Central Asia. The most common camel on Earth, however, is the one-hump Arabian camel, known as the dromedary [DROM-uh-dare-ee] camel.

Have you ever heard that a camel can go long periods of time without drinking "because he stores large amounts of water in his hump"? It is true that a camel can go long periods of time (days or even months) without drinking, but he does not store water in his hump. God made a camel with the ability to store **fat** in his hump. A healthy, well-fed camel can have a hump that weighs as much as 80 pounds. When a camel goes on long journeys (often carrying people or supplies) and food becomes scarce, he relies on stored fat for energy. The longer a camel goes without eating, the more stored fat he uses. At the same time, however, the hump gets smaller and smaller, and often begins to hang off to one side. Later, when the camel is able to get his fill of food again, his hump begins to fill out and goes back to normal.

THE CREATOR'S CONSERVER

How is it that a camel can go days or even months without a drink of water? What have scientists learned about the amazing, God-given design of this water-conserving creature?

First, a camel can get a large amount of the water his body needs from the plants that he eats. This is especially true in the wintertime, when plants hold more moisture than in the summer months. A camel can even get water from eating cacti without hurting his mouth. Can you imagine eating a cactus? A camel can consume such a prickly plant because God gave him a very tough lining in his mouth—so tough that the thorns of a cactus cannot break through the skin.

Second, unlike most animals, a camel loses very little of his water in the form of sweat. God made the camel so that the less water that is available to him, the less he sweats.

Third, camels do not lose great amounts of moisture when they exhale. God designed the nose of a camel with a special mucous that helps to dehydrate (take water out of) much of the moist air coming up from his lungs, recirculating the water throughout his body. Rather than losing great amounts of moisture when he exhales, a camel can conserve as much as 60% of his water.

A final reason that camels can go several days without water in the summertime and several

months without water in the wintertime is because they can drink so much of it when it does happen to be available. A thirsty camel can drink more than 20 gallons of water in only 10 minutes! Remarkably, a camel's stomach may be empty only a few minutes after taking in such a large amount of water. How can this be? Because God designed the camel with billions of small cells that store all of the water so the camel will have it at a later time when water is scarce (such as when he is on a journey through the desert).

Did You Know?

CAMEL STAMINA

Most humans and animals will become sick and die when losing only 10-15% of their body weight in the form of water. Not camels. A camel's journey in the desert may be so long and dry that he can lose 25% of his body weight in water loss, yet still continue on his journey. Amazingly, the camel can keep going because God created him with the capability to use large amounts of water—as much as 40%—from his uniquely designed, long, oval blood cells.

CAMEL-MART

Did you know that camels are kind of like a store? They provide humans with food, clothing, and shelter. Camels can provide milk to drink. They often are killed for their meat. Their skin can be used to make tents. And once a year they shed their hair, which is used for clothing. Recall that John the Baptizer "was clothed in camel's hair" (Matthew 3:4).

Mindless evolution cannot logically explain the wondrous design of the camel. The cool, comical, conserving camel is an amazing creature that testifies to an awesome Creator.

Giraffes Long For A Maker

WHEN
YOU HEAR THE TERM "LONGNECK," an image of a massive, plant-eating dinosaur like *Brachiosaurus* or *Apatosaurus* probably comes to mind. Although these longnecks are now extinct, one impressive, yet funny-looking, longneck is still around—the giraffe. Giraffes are not reptiles, but mammals whose necks are longer and heavier than the average man.

An adult male giraffe's neck can reach lengths of six feet and weigh as much as 600 pounds. You might think that the giraffe's neck must have many more bones (called vertebrae) than humans, since its neck is so much longer than ours. Actually, the

Adult Male Giraffes can grow to Heights of 18 Feet.

giraffe has the same number of bones in its neck as humans and other mammals—seven. The difference—each neck vertebrae of a giraffe can be as long as 10 inches.

More remarkable than the length and weight of a giraffe's neck is its internal design. For example, in order for a giraffe to get blood to travel up the eight feet from its heart to its brain, a giraffe's heart must pump extremely hard. In fact, the blood pressure of a giraffe is about twice that of any other large mammal and as much as three times that of the average person.

But what about when a giraffe suddenly lowers its head several feet below its heart to get a drink of water? What happens to all of the blood that the heart normally pumps upward against gravity to the brain? If the design of the giraffe were merely left up to time and chance (as evolution teaches), what would you expect to happen the first time a giraffe tried to lower its neck to get a drink of water? It would seem the heart would pump so much blood to the brain that its blood vessels would explode, or its brain would fill up with blood so quickly that the giraffe would pass out.

So how does the giraffe keep from having brain bleeds or from feeling woozy and passing out every time it bends down and raises back up? Giraffes are specially designed with valves in their large neck artery. These valves help control how much blood gets to the brain during those times when the giraffe has its head lowered.

So how did these valves come about? Who designed giraffes so masterfully? The intelligent Designer, of course. On day six of Creation, God made the longneck mammal we call a giraffe.

GIRAFFES MAY LOOK CLUMSY AND SLOW, BUT WHEN THEY NEED TO, THEY CAN REALLY RUN. ONE GIRAFFE WAS CLOCKED RUNNING A SHORT DISTANCE AT MORE THAN 30 MILES PER HOUR.

GIRAFFES NOT ONLY HAVE LONG NECKS. THEY ALSO HAVE...

LONG LEGS
The legs of a giraffe are about the same length as its neck—about six feet long.

LONG TAILS
Even though the giraffe is famous for its long neck, it also has a very long tail. In fact, it has the longest tail of any land animal living today, growing up to eight feet long. A giraffe uses its tail to keep flies and other insects away.

LONG TONGUES
A giraffe uses its 18-inch tongue to grasp twigs and strip them of leaves. The tongues of giraffes are also incredibly nimble, able to "lick up" leaves from in-between the thorns of acacia trees.

LONG HEARTS
A giraffe's heart must be large enough to pump blood eight feet upward to its brain. Whereas the human heart is about the size of a clinched fist and weighs less than one pound, the heart of a giraffe can be two feet long and weigh more than 20 pounds.

LONG BABIES
When a baby giraffe is born, it drops about six feet straight to the ground. Normally, it gets to its feet in less than an hour, already standing six feet tall.

GIRAFFES HAVE BIG HOOVES (12 INCHES ACROSS) AND A SUPER STRONG KICK.

The "King of Beasts" Calls for a Creator

I HAVE ALWAYS LIKED LIONS. NOT THAT I ENJOY PETTING OR PLAYING WITH LIONS, BUT I HAVE ALWAYS ENJOYED watching and talking about these amazing cats. Admittedly, part of my affection for lions comes from the fact that my last name is Lyons (pronounced "lions"). I am also partial toward lions because my favorite school—and the one from which I graduated—has a lion as its mascot. In addition, the lion is special to me and millions of Christians around the world because the Bible calls the Lord Jesus "the lion of the tribe of Judah" (Revelation 5:5).

Evolutionists would have us believe that the first lion evolved through purely natural processes approximately 25 million years ago. However, no proof exists for such evolution. Cats (both big and small) certainly have changed over time (after all, lions and tigers can mate and have "ligers"). But there is no proof that lions came from a totally different kind of animal 25 million years ago. Everything we see in nature (including the existence of big cats like lions) is reasonably understood in light of what the Bible teaches: "in six days the Lord made the heavens and the earth, the sea, and all that is in them" (Exodus 20:11). Furthermore, the first chapter of Genesis clearly states that on the sixth day of Creation, "God made the beast of the earth according to its kind" (1:25). Lions fit into the biblical category of "beasts."

LIONS DO NOT ACTUALLY LIVE IN JUNGLES, BUT IN AFRICA'S SAVANNAS, SOUTH OF THE SAHARA DESERT.

The lion is often called the "king of the jungle" or the "king of beasts," because it is the most famous and feared of the big cats. It is not the largest cat on Earth (that honor belongs to the Siberian tiger), but it still is one of the most fearsome. Lions can grow to be 10 feet long, 4 feet high, and weigh as much as 550 pounds. Female lions (called lionesses) are not as large as the males, but even they can reach 300 pounds. Perhaps most frightening of all is the lion's heart-rattling roar, which reportedly can be heard from as much as five miles away.

Many people get to see tame lions at circuses. Amazingly, trainers have taught these large, fearsome cats to leap over hurdles, walk on their back legs, give high fives, and jump through hoops of fire. How can people train such fearsome cats? Part of the answer is found in Genesis 1:27-28. God said that He made man in His image, which allows man to "have dominion over the fish of the sea, over the birds of the air, and over the cattle, over all the earth and over every creeping thing that creeps on the earth." In fact, He commanded man to "subdue" the creation and "have dominion…over every living thing that moves on the earth."

Lions are not normally very active during the daytime. In fact, lions are known to sleep about 20 hours a day. Most of their hunting takes place at night. Interestingly, the males are generally not part of the hunting and killing of prey. That job is mainly left up to the lionesses, while the males, in turn, provide protection for the lionesses. When hunting in groups (called prides), lions have been known to attack very large animals such as hippos and even elephants.

The mane of a male lion serves at least two known purposes: (1) It makes the lion look bigger—and thus more likely to deter intruders from the pride; and (2) It can help soften the blows from an enemy—normally another lion who wanders into his territory and challenges his authority.

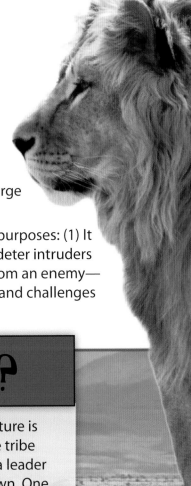

Did You Know?

The first time the term "lion" is used in Scripture is Genesis 49:9. There Jacob prophesies that the tribe of Judah will grow from being a lion's cub to a leader before whom the other tribes would bow down. One of the final times in Scripture in which the term "lion" is used is in reference to Jesus, "the lion of the tribe of Judah" (Revelation 5:5). Indeed, Jesus was the strong and powerful, prophesied descendant of Judah, Who conquered death and brought eternal life to those who will submit to Him.

The ENORMOUS
did NOT

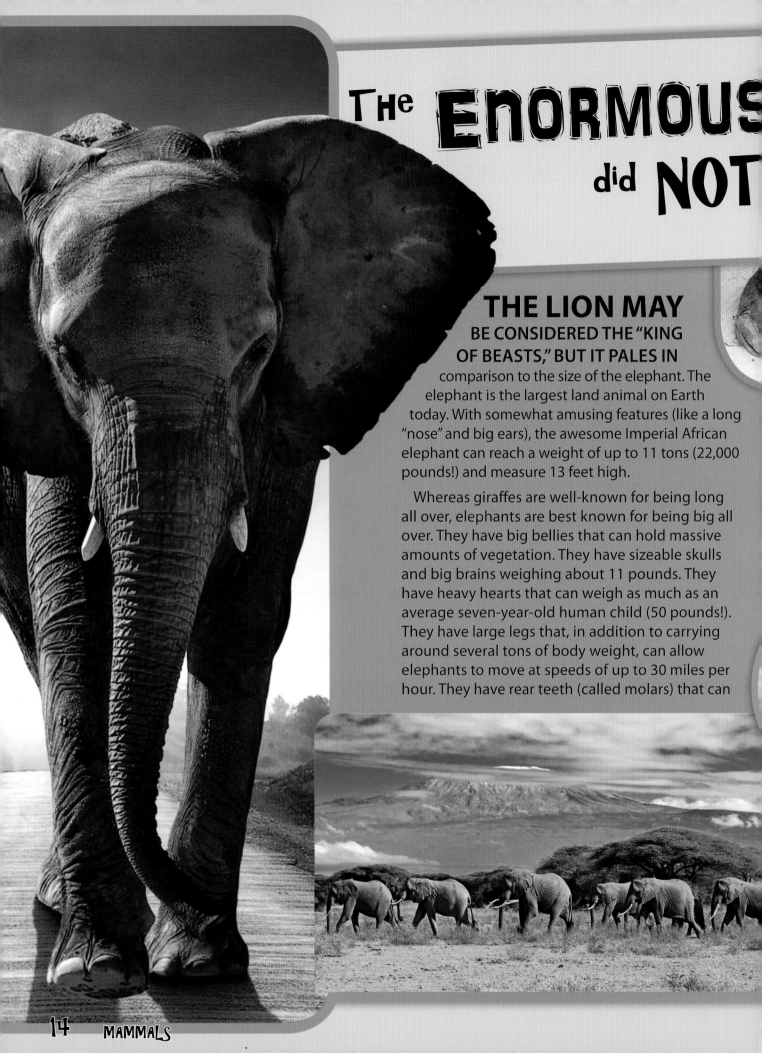

THE LION MAY BE CONSIDERED THE "KING OF BEASTS," BUT IT PALES IN comparison to the size of the elephant. The elephant is the largest land animal on Earth today. With somewhat amusing features (like a long "nose" and big ears), the awesome Imperial African elephant can reach a weight of up to 11 tons (22,000 pounds!) and measure 13 feet high.

Whereas giraffes are well-known for being long all over, elephants are best known for being big all over. They have big bellies that can hold massive amounts of vegetation. They have sizeable skulls and big brains weighing about 11 pounds. They have heavy hearts that can weigh as much as an average seven-year-old human child (50 pounds!). They have large legs that, in addition to carrying around several tons of body weight, can allow elephants to move at speeds of up to 30 miles per hour. They have rear teeth (called molars) that can

ELEPHANT EVOLVE

This flexible, funny-looking, boneless flesh is not the result of random, evolutionary accidents as some would have us believe. Logic demands that mindless, random happenstances could never cause such an amazing organ to come about. There is no evidence for the evolution of the elephant's trunk.

grow to be one foot long and weigh 10 pounds. Their tusks, which are actually long teeth, can grow to be 10 feet long and weigh 200 pounds. Even their skin is "big." It can grow to be up to one-inch thick in certain places. (Can you imagine having skin that thick?) Elephants even have big babies, which can weigh as much as 250 pounds at birth. The fact is, the African elephant is several times larger than the average dinosaur, which was about the size of a large cow.

The elephant is perhaps most well-known for the six-foot-long, 300-pound trunk hanging from its face. Scientists believe that the elephant's trunk is "the most versatile organ in the animal kingdom." It is made up of 100,000 muscle units. Some muscles run longways, up and down the trunk. Other muscles radiate around each nostril, similar to the spokes on a bicycle.

The elephant can use his trunk to lift things three times the trunk's weight. An elephant with a 300-pound trunk could lift a 900-pound cow.

The elephant uses his trunk to suck, pour, and spray water into his mouth and on his body. He picks up food with it and tosses or blows it into his mouth. When he swims, he can use it as a snorkel. When he has an eye itch, he wipes his eye with it. And when he gets mad, he can use his trunk in a fight.

DID YOU KNOW?

One elephant easily could kill a man simply by stepping on him with one foot or by striking him with his powerful trunk. Yet, for thousands of years, humans have been known to live with, and even tame, these massive beasts. Over 2,200 years ago, the empire of Carthage, led by its legendary general, Hannibal, used tame African elephants to cross the Swiss Alps and battle the Romans. Today, many elephants are still being controlled by man. Tamed elephants are used in various Asian countries in religious ceremonies, or to do physical labor like hauling lumber or transporting people from place to place. Elephants also are frequently seen performing at circuses. Amazing, is it not, that humans have trained these creatures—which can outweigh them by as much as 22,000 pounds—to perform some of the same tricks we train dogs to perform? Why do you think humans are able to train these colossal creatures? For the same reason humans have been able to train lions, tigers, and bears (read Genesis 1:26-28).

Elephants can move at speeds of up to 30 miles per hour.

? HAVE YOU CONSIDERED....?

SCRIPTURE'S WAY OF SORTING ANIMALS

Everyone has a way of sorting things. You might sort your shirts in one drawer and your pants in another. Or you might have them all mixed up in different drawers. You might arrange your clothes in your closet by kind, color, or size. It may be that you arrange the books on your desk by author, subject, or title. You might also sort volumes by the year the books were published or the year that you read the books. The fact is, there are all kinds of ways of sorting things, including sorting animals.

Most people today categorize animals into one of five major groups: mammals, reptiles, amphibians, fish, and birds. But the way we usually sort animals is not the only way to classify animals. Consider the way that God categorized animals in Scripture. In the very first chapter of the Bible, God divided animals into very basic, natural groups. Instead of creating all of the mammals on one day and all of the reptiles on another, He made animals that swim and fly on day five and land animals on day six (Genesis 1:20-23,24-25). Thus, in addition to the fish He made on day five, He created other water-living creatures, including mammals, like whales, and reptiles, such as plesiosaurs. What's more, birds were not the only flying things He made on day five. On this day, God also made the only flying mammal alive today (the bat), as well as all of the extinct flying reptiles (such as *Pteranodon* and *Pterodactyl*).

The book of Leviticus expands on God's classification of animals. In chapter 11, God instructed the Israelites about "clean" and "unclean" animals. As He listed these animals, God divided the creatures into land animals, water animals, and flying things (including birds, bats, and flying insects). As at Creation, God did not divide animals into mammals, birds, fish, reptiles, and amphibians. Rather, God categorized animals in a very easy-to-understand, natural way. He sorted animals more according to the animals' locomotion (do they fly, swim, or walk?) and environment (do they inhabit the air, water, or land?), instead of whether or not they have hair, lay eggs, or nurse their young.

Just remember, although it can be helpful to learn how we classify animals today, the Bible's classification of animals is also very logical. Best of all, it is easy to remember.

THE BLUE WHALE IS NO FLUKE OF EVOLUTION

A 19-foot-tall skull of a blue whale

THERE IS BIG—AND THEN THERE IS THE BLUE WHALE. ELEPHANTS ARE BIG, BUT THEY AREN'T

"blue whale big." Even though *Argentinosaurus*—the largest dinosaur man has ever discovered—was huge (an estimated 100 tons or 200,000 pounds), it still was only about half the size of the largest known blue whale.

Blue whales are born big and then become enormous. Baby blue whales (called calves) are almost 25 feet long at birth and weigh as much as a small pick-up truck (6,000 pounds). The calf feeds on her mother's rich milk and gains a whopping 200 pounds **every day** during the first year of her life. By the time the baby becomes a full-grown whale, she can reach 100 feet in length and weigh nearly 200 tons or 400,000 pounds.

Blue whales have a fluke (tail) used to propel them

forward under water. This fluke is wider than a racquetball court. Their tongue is so large that 50 people can stand on it at one time. Their heart is the size of a small car, and they have blood vessels large enough for small fish to swim through. (Not that fish do; that's just how large these whales' blood vessels are.) The blue whale's largest blood vessel (called the aorta) is so large that a small person could actually crawl through it.

Can you believe that evolutionists claim that blue whales evolved from land animals? Supposedly a small, fox-like creature began eating fish and started living more and more of its life in the water. Over millions of years, allegedly, this animal's front legs became flippers, its back legs all but disappeared, its tail became a fluke, and it began living full-time in the oceans. Where is the proof for such a story? Actually, there is no proof—there is only evolutionists' interpretation of various fossils they have found in the ground. The fact is, no one has ever proved (or will ever prove) that the blue whale's great-great-great…granddaddy was a fox-like land animal.

Whereas humans and most land animals could survive for only a few minutes in the frigid waters that marine mammals call home, God designed whales perfectly for life in the sea. The blue whale is able to withstand bitterly cold water temperatures because of the tens of thousands of pounds of blubber in its body. This blubber, which is made up mostly of fat, functions as insulation, helping keep the whale from freezing to death in chilly waters. What's more, when krill (shrimp-like creatures that whales feed on) are scarce, blue whales can live off of the energy stored in their blubber.

Does it really make sense to believe that a fox-like land animal evolved into a whale over millions of years? How did it evolve the many specialized features of whales, such as the capability to withstand freezing cold temperatures? How did its nose move to the top of its head and become a blowhole? How did the mother whale (called a cow) evolve the necessary ability to pump her rich milk into the mouth of her baby, rather than simply allow the calf to suck in the milk as land mammals do? (If calves had to try to suck 200 pounds of milk a day, they would likely suck in a lot of water and die.) How did the supposed fox-like ancestor of whales evolve the ability to endure the extreme water pressure that whales feel when they dive hundreds or thousands of feet below the surface? Such pressure would kill most animals.

Neither the blue whale nor any other whale evolved these incredible, specialized features. No fox-like creature fathered these amazing animals. God designed these wonderful whales to live in water. The Bible says that on the fifth day of Creation, "God created great sea creatures and every living thing that moves, with which the water abounded, according to their kind" (Genesis 1:21).

A BLUE WHALE FEEDING, WITH POUCH INFLATED

WWW.NATUREPL.COM

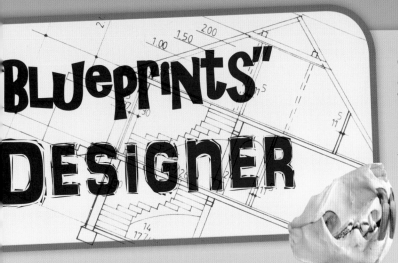

BLUEPRINTS" DESIGNER

ARCHITECTS MAKE BLUEPRINTS, WHICH ARE THEN USED TO BUILD HOUSES OR OFFICE BUILDINGS.

Coaches work up "blueprints" when they come up with creative game plans in the hopes of a victory. Military leaders work up a "blueprint" as they form a plan of attack prior to going into battle. Blueprints are designs. Architects, coaches, military leaders, and many others often form various kinds of blueprints prior to building a house, a team, or an army. Most everyone understands the value of blueprints, as well as the fact that blueprints call for a creator. Blueprints do not come together by time, chance, and non-intelligence. Furthermore, the more complex the designs, the more intelligent the designer(s) must be.

Have you ever considered the design of the beaver? In a sense, a beaver's body is the result of a magnificent blueprint. Its tail was made according to a blueprint. And it has a kind of blueprint engrained in its brain that enables it to build complex dams and dwellings.

The beaver has one of the most recognized tails in the world. It is long and flat, which helps the beaver to balance when it stands on its hind legs. As a beaver swims, it uses its tail like a boat's rudder, to steer exactly where it needs to go. When a beaver senses danger, it can make a loud noise by slapping its tail on the water, which alerts other beavers to get away and hide. Does it make good sense to think that a perfectly designed, balancing, boat-like rudder, which also functions as an alarm device, grew by chance on the end of the beaver's body? To ask is to answer. Like a blueprint, the beaver's useful, versatile tail shows design, forethought, intent, and purpose.

In addition to the beaver's amazing tail, these cute critters are also well-known for their four incisors (front teeth). Beavers use their strong jaws and sturdy teeth to cut down small trees to build dams and homes. Their teeth continue to grow throughout their lives, but they never grow too long since the teeth are constantly wearing down as the beavers use them to cut and gnaw wood.

Beavers not only have perfectly designed teeth; they also have perfectly designed mouths. The beaver's front four teeth are separated from its back 16 teeth by a large space. (The front teeth are used for cutting and the back teeth for grinding.) In this space are flaps of skin that can close—separating the front teeth and back teeth. By closing up its mouth behind its incisors, the beaver can haul or gnaw on wood in the water without getting water in its mouth. The flaps of skin also help keep splinters out of the beaver's mouth. The beaver's amazing teeth and mouth demand a Designer and defy the false theory of evolution.

Not only is the beaver itself a kind of blueprint, it also has the ability to work from a blueprint. This blueprint is "built" into the brain of beavers. We call this instinct. A family of beavers will spend weeks or months purposefully placing branches, leaves, stones, and mud in specific places in order to build useful dams and lodges. Beavers are animal architects that demand an adequate explanation. They do not have to attend engineering school to know how to build a dam. They instinctively know how to raise water levels by building dams.

How can anyone study the beaver and come to the conclusion that this animal is merely the result of mindless matter? Such functional, complex engineering demands a Chief Engineer. Indeed, beavers'"blueprints" call for a Creator.

THe PUZZLING PLatYPUS iS No PRODUCt of EVOLUTION

With its broad, flat tail, the platypus (like the beaver) can maneuver easily in water. It also stores fat in its tail: normally, the fuller the tail, the healthier the platypus.

SCIENTISTS CLASSIFY

THE PLATYPUS AS A MAMMAL, YET IT IS UNLIKE ANY OTHER MAMMAL YOU have ever seen. It is about the size of a house cat with fur thicker than a polar bear's. It can store food in its mouth like a chipmunk. It has a beaver-like tail and webbed feet like an otter. It has a bill like a duck and spurs like a rooster. What's more, it lays eggs like a turtle and produces venom like a snake. If there was ever an animal to call "unique," it would be the platypus.

Platypuses show every indication of being designed by the grand Designer.

• God designed their feet to work extremely well both in water and on land. They flatten

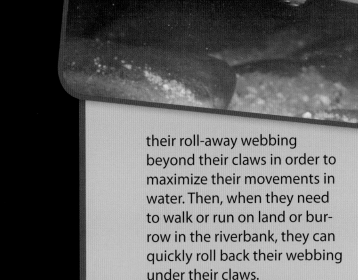

their roll-away webbing beyond their claws in order to maximize their movements in water. Then, when they need to walk or run on land or burrow in the riverbank, they can quickly roll back their webbing under their claws.

- God gave the platypus thick fur to stay warm in cold waters. A platypus has about 800 hairs per square millimeter of skin (compared to the human who has about two hairs per square millimeter on his head). The platypus's fur is so dense that it can trap a layer of air next to its skin. This air works as insulation to keep the platypus warm.

THiS iS tHe SizE oF oNe square MiLLiMeter

- How can the platypus completely close its eyes and ears under water and find enough food to survive? Does it just clumsily tumble bill-

first into the bottoms of rivers and streams in hopes of getting lucky? Actually, God designed this curious creature with a very sensitive snout. Scientists have learned that the platypus's leathery bill has a complex electro-receptor system in it. This system allows the platypus to sense the weak electric impulses in the muscles of its prey, including earthworms, tadpoles, and shrimp, which often are hiding under the mud and rocks.

Like so many animals that scientists study, the more scientists learn about the platypus, the more amazed they are at this curious creature. Although evolutionists would have us believe that this unique animal is the product of many millions of years of evolution, in reality, the duck-billed platypus declares the glory of God.

"You are worthy, O Lord, to receive glory and honor and power; for You created all things, and by Your will they exist and were created" (Revelation 4:11).

? HaVE YoU CoNSIDERED....?

MaMMaLS, REPTILES, aND THE FOSSIL RECORD

Evolutionists have long taught that mammals evolved millions of years after the reptiles. And once mammals came onto the scene, allegedly millions of years after the dinosaurs supposedly evolved, all the mammals were "small, mostly about mouse-sized, and rare." In fact, we are told that for the first 150 million years of their existence, mammals "were never able to get beyond little rat-like things."

But as so often is the case, when more evidence is gathered, evolutionary "facts" become outright errors. A few years ago, the fossils of a mammal "20 times larger" than what evolutionists believed to be possible were reported to be in the same fossil beds as the dinosaurs. Another fossilized mammal discovered in the same area actually had the remains of a five-inch dinosaur in its stomach. What does this prove? Only that mammals much larger than "little ratlike things" not only lived with dinosaurs, but even ate some of them.

One year after scientists reported about the dinosaur-eating mammal, another mammal fossil find was revealed. This time it was of a furry, beaver-like animal. What was so special about this mammal? Evolutionists confessed that the animal lived long before they previously thought such swimming mammals lived—even before many of the dinosaurs lived.

For about 100 years, science textbooks, museum exhibits, and many movies taught that the mammals which lived with dinosaurs were very small, about the size of a shrew. Yet just a few fossil discoveries in the last few years have overturned all that evolutionary scientists formerly thought about mammals and dinosaurs.

Evolutionists are wrong about the origins and development of mammals. Mammals did not evolve from reptiles, nor were the small or the large mammals separated in time from the dinosaurs by many millions of years. As the Bible teaches, and as these few fossil discoveries have shown, the theory of evolution is based on unproven assump-

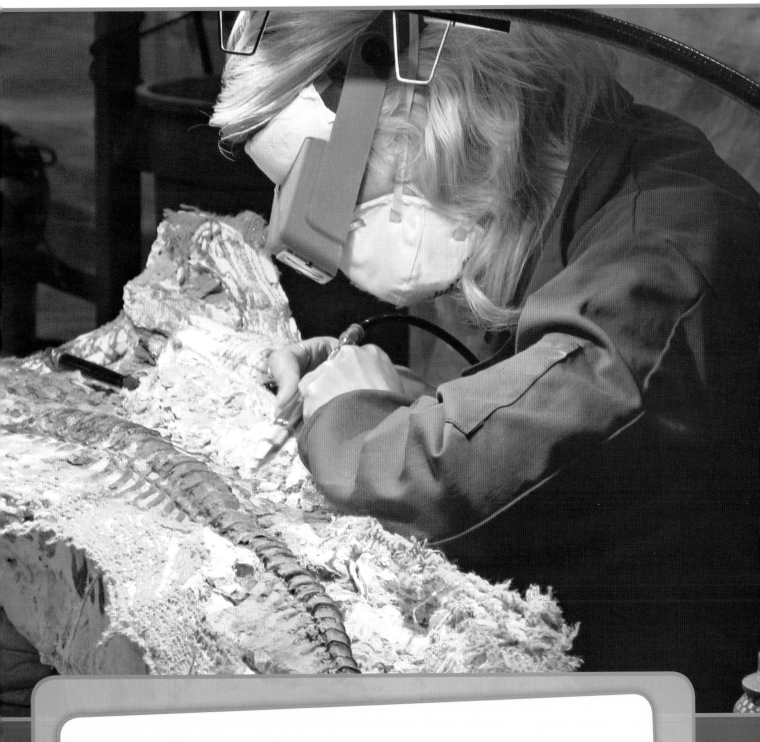

tions, incorrect calculations, and extremely exaggerated periods of time. The truth is, God created mammals, reptiles, and all other animals only a few thousand years ago on the fifth and sixth days of Creation.

REP†ILES

2

GOD MADE A VARIETY OF REPTILES ON THE FIFTH AND SIXTH DAYS OF CREATION. ON DAY FIVE, HE CREATED MARINE REPTILES, SUCH AS SEA SNAKES AND SEA

turtles, as well as extinct, flying reptiles, such as *Pteranodon* and *Pterodactyl* (Genesis 1:20-23). On day six, God created "everything that creeps on the earth" (Genesis 1:25), including reptiles such as cobras, geckos, and Komodo dragons. Unlike mammals, but similar to amphibians, such as frogs and salamanders, reptiles are cold-blood animals, meaning their body temperature changes as the outside temperature changes. (Reptiles depend on the Sun and warm surfaces to raise their body temperature.) In contrast to amphibians, reptiles normally have dry, tough skin (made of scales, shields, or plates) and lay eggs with hard, leathery shells. As with all other groups of animals on Earth, reptiles provide excellent testimony to the existence and glory of their Creator.

Superbly
Designed Snakes

WHEN MOST PEOPLE HEAR THE WORD
"SNAKE," THEY QUICKLY BECOME UNNERVED. SNAKES' WAGGLING, FORKED TONGUE, BEADY EYES, AND SLITHERING BODIES GENERALLY disturb people. And although most snakes are not venomous, the fact that some of them are leads many people to avoid them all together. The truth is, however, snakes are superb examples of design in the animal kingdom.

SNAKES HAVE FORKED TONGUES. A FORKED TONGUE ALLOWS THEM TO SENSE FROM WHICH DIRECTION A SMELL IS COMING.

Masterful Movements

Evolutionists claim that snakes evolved from lizard-like ancestors that lost their legs over the course of millions of years. However, no real proof exists for this far-fetched theory. The fact is, snakes, with their long, skinny, **legless** bodies, are perfectly designed to move efficiently on all sorts of surfaces. They can climb **up** trees, **in** trees, and **down** trees. They can slither underground or aboveground and over hard rock or loose sand. Some snakes, such as anacondas (the largest snakes in the world), are excellent swimmers. Other snakes, like flying tree snakes, can effectively jump and glide from one tree to another or from the tree to the ground. The movement of snakes is a marvelous thing to witness. They clearly have been designed with a powerful, complex muscular system, which is perfectly attached to hundreds of bones—all of which allow snakes to bend, curl, twist, and turn in all sorts of ways and on all kinds of terrain.

Sensational Sensors

Have you ever seen a night vision camera with specially designed sensors that are built to detect heat? Soldiers often use this technology (called infrared) when they need to move around in the dark while keeping a close eye on the enemy. What these soldiers actually see with infrared equipment is the heat of various objects, including humans and animals.

Amazingly, some snakes have built-in, heat-sensitive pits that are located on the top of their mouths, just below their nostrils. With these, snakes are able to sense the presence of both prey and predators. These pits are not merely empty holes in their heads. They are actually complex organs packed with nerve endings that snakes use to accurately detect the direction and distance of other animals. Question: If no one would ever claim that infrared cameras are the result of the non-intelligent, random processes of evolution, why would anyone say that the superb heat sensors of snakes are merely the product of evolution?

Did You Know?

Some snakes have fangs from which they inject a poison called venom. Venomous snakes, such as the King Cobra, produce the poison in small sacs behind their eyes.

When these snakes bite their prey, venom is released through their hollow teeth. This action is similar to the way a doctor uses a needle to inject medicine into a patient.

If no one thinks that a doctor's needle is the product of evolution, why would anyone think that evolution could explain a snake's "natural needles"? God designed both their fangs and their venom production abilities.

RATTLESNAKES MAY BE BEST KNOWN FOR THEIR RATTLES, BUT THEY ALSO HAVE AMAZING HEAT-SENSITIVE PITS. GOD GAVE THESE SNAKES SUCH WELL-DESIGNED, INFRARED SENSORS THAT THEY CAN DETECT CHANGES IN TEMPERATURE AS LITTLE AS 1/1000TH OF A DEGREE.

SNAKES USE THEIR VENOM TO PARALYZE OR KILL THEIR PREY. MAN HAS DISCOVERED VARIOUS USES FOR SNAKE VENOM, INCLUDING USING IT IN CERTAIN MEDICINES AND MEDICAL RESEARCH.

Superbly Designed Snakes are also Known for their...

Plastic Man, Mr. Fantastic, and all other stretchy superheroes are the inventions of creative imaginations. Snakes, on the other hand, are the **real** deal when it comes to elasticity.

It is difficult for humans to swallow anything much bigger than a quarter, yet some snakes (like African Rock Pythons) can stretch their jaws and swallow prey as big as a 130-pound deer—horns, hooves, and all. How can a snake swallow prey so much bigger than its own head? If left up to evolution, one would think that the first time a snake tried consuming such a large animal he would choke to death. The truth is, God designed snakes with very stretchy ligaments that allow them to separate their jaws and open their mouths extremely wide.

"God made…everything that creeps on the ground" (Genesis 1:25).

A snake's scales, sensors, fangs, elastic ligaments, and versatile movements testify to something greater than "millions of years of evolution." These wonders of design demand a Designer; they declare His glory.

KOMODO DRAGONS take a Bite out of EVOLUTION

KOMODO DRAGONS

LIVE IN INDONESIA ON THE ISLANDS OF KOMODO AND FLORES, AS WELL AS A few other nearby islands. These reptiles are the heaviest living lizards in the world. They can reach 10 feet in length and weigh over 250 pounds. They have thick skin, powerful legs, lashing tails, tough toes, and sharp claws. Such physical characteristics allow komodos to kill animals that are several times their size, including water buffaloes.

Komodo dragons do not breathe fire, but they do have an eerie forked tongue and a vicious bite. Komodos have very sharp teeth—a total of 60—that they use to tear their prey apart. They can swallow large pieces of flesh at a time. In only a few minutes, a 100-pound Komodo can eat 80 pounds of meat.

Unlike humans, Komodos do not mind leftover pieces of food in their teeth. In fact, these leftover food particles promote the growth of deadly bacteria in the Komodo's mouth. Why would any Komodo want deadly bacteria living in its mouth? When a Komodo bites its prey, often times just once, those bacteria cause an infection in the prey, making the bite deadly. The bacteria begin to sicken and weaken the prey, eventually killing it in a few days. Amazingly, the bacteria do not harm the Komodo.

Evolution cannot logically explain the existence of this amazing animal. Why do the bacteria harm the Komodo's prey, but not the Komodo itself? How could the Komodo have evolved the ability to carry deadly bacteria in its mouth without first killing itself? If evolution is true, why did the first Komodo not die from these deadly bacteria before producing offspring? The bacteria-filled bite of the Komodo is a puzzle for those who think these animals evolved from earlier reptiles, which could not have survived with such bacteria growing in their mouths. Creationists, however, realize that Komodos came from the Creator on day six of Creation (Genesis 1:24-25).

THE GECKO DECLARES GOD'S GLORY

much as 50% of their body weight in insects, including cockroaches, crickets, and beetles. Geckos can be great to have around the house or at work. At Apologetics Press, where this book was published, we have several geckos that often hunt insects just outside the front door. We welcome these little insect-ingesting critters that remind us of God's creative designs and power.

Many species of geckos also have an amazing escape maneuver when caught by the tail by predators. Geckos don't play dead or become invisible; they actually self-amputate their tails. If a predator catches a gecko by the tail, the lizard contracts its tail muscles in such a way that a tail bone (called a vertebra) breaks. Thus, the gecko is able to get away, while the predator is left holding the detached part of the tail. Amazingly, over the next few months the gecko grows a new tail, complete with tough tissue, muscles, and scales.

Imagine if cars could regenerate themselves after accidents. What if cell phones could automatically restore themselves after being smashed? If an engi-

YOU MAY THINK

THAT GECKOS ARE MERELY CUTE, LITTLE LIZARDS THAT OCCASIONALLY APPEAR IN CAR INSURANCE commercials, but the truth is that these remarkable reptiles are loaded with design. In a way, they are like miniature superheroes that can take out pests, escape danger, and walk up walls.

When you have an insect pest problem, who do you call? Most people call an exterminator who sprays chemicals and sets out glue boards in hopes of ridding your house of pests. Perhaps everyone should just invest in some of God's geckos. After all, these little reptiles are known to eat in one night as

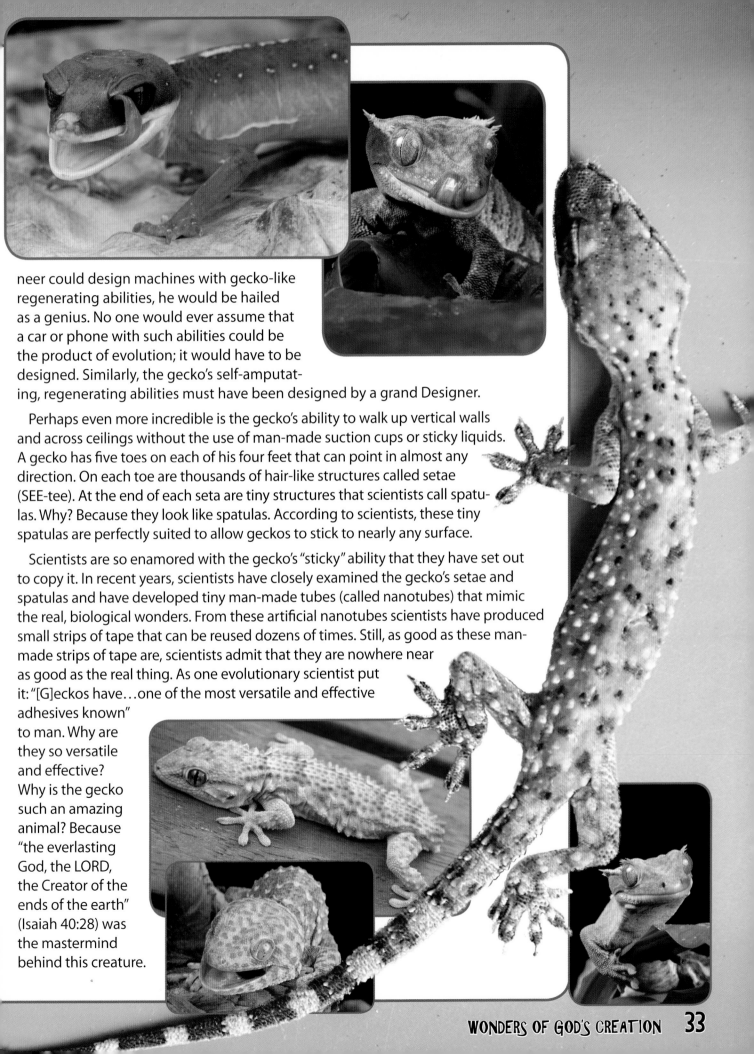

neer could design machines with gecko-like regenerating abilities, he would be hailed as a genius. No one would ever assume that a car or phone with such abilities could be the product of evolution; it would have to be designed. Similarly, the gecko's self-amputating, regenerating abilities must have been designed by a grand Designer.

Perhaps even more incredible is the gecko's ability to walk up vertical walls and across ceilings without the use of man-made suction cups or sticky liquids. A gecko has five toes on each of his four feet that can point in almost any direction. On each toe are thousands of hair-like structures called setae (SEE-tee). At the end of each seta are tiny structures that scientists call spatulas. Why? Because they look like spatulas. According to scientists, these tiny spatulas are perfectly suited to allow geckos to stick to nearly any surface.

Scientists are so enamored with the gecko's "sticky" ability that they have set out to copy it. In recent years, scientists have closely examined the gecko's setae and spatulas and have developed tiny man-made tubes (called nanotubes) that mimic the real, biological wonders. From these artificial nanotubes scientists have produced small strips of tape that can be reused dozens of times. Still, as good as these man-made strips of tape are, scientists admit that they are nowhere near as good as the real thing. As one evolutionary scientist put it: "[G]eckos have…one of the most versatile and effective adhesives known" to man. Why are they so versatile and effective? Why is the gecko such an amazing animal? Because "the everlasting God, the LORD, the Creator of the ends of the earth" (Isaiah 40:28) was the mastermind behind this creature.

? Have You Considered...?

PEOPLE, PETS, AND PRIORITIES: A PROPER VIEW OF ANIMALS

A pet can be a wonderful thing. Many people have dogs or cats as pets. Some people have pet snakes or lizards. Others have parrots or parakeets. More exotic pets include monkeys, sugar gliders, and alligators. Personally, I've always loved dogs. I have fond memories of all the dogs I've ever owned, just as you likely have pleasant thoughts of past or present pets. They keep us company when we are alone. They may help calm us when we are stressed. They may even lift our spirits when we are sad. Pets can be wonderful to own for a variety of reasons.

We need to be careful, however, not to think more of pets than we should. Though dogs may be "man's best friend," we must keep in mind that dogs are just animals. They are not created in the "image of God" as humans are (Genesis 1:26-28), and they do not have an immortal soul as humans have (Matthew 10:28; Luke 16:19-31). Although we may become very attached to our pets, we must keep in mind that the value of an animal, whether a pet gecko, a Golden Retriever, or a parrot in no way compares to that of a human (Matthew 6:26).

Whereas many people seem to put their love and admiration for pets on nearly the same level as their affection for people, God does not give animals such value. For example, one Bible encyclopedia called *International Standard Bible Encyclopedia* summed up the Bible's references to one of man's favorite pets (dogs) in the following way: "References to the dog, both in the Old Testament and in the New Testament, are usually of a contemptuous character. A dog, and especially a dead dog, is used as a figure of insignificance." Simply put, the Bible teaches that human life is inherently more valuable than animal life.

As early as Genesis chapter one, God revealed that humans are on a higher level than the rest of God's creation.

Then God said, "Let Us make man in Our image, according to Our likeness; let them have **dominion** over the fish of the sea, over the birds of the air, and over the cattle, **over all the earth** and over every creeping thing that creeps on the earth…." Then

God blessed them, and God said to them, "Be fruitful and multiply; fill the earth and **subdue** it; have **dominion** over the fish of the sea, over the birds of the air, and **over every living thing that moves on the earth**" (Genesis 1:26,28).

Since the time of Adam and Eve, God gave His image-bearers (humans) the right to rule over all of the creation. Until Jesus returns and this world is burned up (2 Peter 3:10), God has given man permission to use His creation in order to survive and flourish. In addition to the rocks, minerals, and vegetation that God made for man's benefit, God told Noah that all animals "are given into your hand. **Every moving thing that lives shall be food for you. I have given you all things, even as the green herbs**" (Genesis 9:2-3).

Man has not only been given permission from God to train and work animals, and to kill animals for clothing or sacrifices (Genesis 3:21; 4:4), but also to eat animals—including all kinds of pets. As hard as this is for some Americans to admit, dogs, cats, and all other pets are every bit as much an animal as cows, chickens, and pigs.

In America, it is common to eat cows. In other countries (especially India), it can be offensive to eat cows. At the same time, the eating of dog meat is very common in certain cultures. In fact, some people around the world raise dogs like many Americans raise cows, for the sole purpose of selling them as meat.

Although I don't plan on eating dog or cat meat anytime soon, sometimes we need to be reminded that even though dogs, cats, and other animals can make great pets, they are still **just animals**. They are a part of God's amazing creation that He gave for man to responsibly subdue, rule over, and, if need be, even eat.

Painting by Lewis Lavoie

"FEARFULLY GREAT REPTILES"

PERHAPS THE MOST

FAMOUS REPTILES ARE THOSE THAT NO LONGER LIVE ON EARTH. WE CALL THEM DINOSAURS.

The word "dinosaur" comes from two Greek words: *deinos*, meaning "fearfully great," and *saurus*, meaning "reptile" or "lizard." Since 1842 when a scientist by the name of Richard Owen coined the term, man has referred to certain extinct reptiles (known from the fossil record and history) as dinosaurs.

Certain dinosaurs were the longest and largest reptiles ever to roam the Earth. *Apatosaurus*, more popularly known as *Brontosaurus*, was taller than a giraffe, longer than four cars, and heavier than five large elephants. In 1986, scientists unearthed the remains of another large dinosaur they named *Seismosaurus*, meaning "earthquake lizard." Scientists estimated that when this reptile died its length measured 120 feet from head to tail.

The heaviest dinosaur ever known to live was discovered in Argentina in 1991. Scientists named the animal simply *Argentinosaurus*. Just one of its backbones, called vertebrae,

measured five feet, while one of its rib bones was 14 feet long. Scientists estimate that *Argentinosaurus* reached a weight of over 100 tons (or 200,000 pounds)—as much as **55** average cars!

Scientists are puzzled about how creatures this large could have eaten enough to survive. They are not even sure how such a large animal could pump blood up to its head. Those who believe in evolution wonder what caused dinosaurs to reach such giant sizes. These interesting questions simply point us back to the amazing wisdom and power of God. Evolution didn't make *Seismosaurus*, *Argentinosaurus*, or any other reptiles from the past or present—God did! We can be sure that God had no problem creating these marvelous creatures with amazing blood circulation abilities. Nor did He have difficulty feeding them. Nothing is too hard for God (Jeremiah 32:17,27). "The Lord made the heavens and the earth, the sea, and all that is in them" (Exodus 20:11), including the dinosaurs and their habitat.

"LOOK NOW at the BEHEMOTH"

Painting by Lewis Lavoie

Whose tail was so massive it swayed "like a cedar" (Job 40:17).

GOD ONCE SPOKE TO

JOB ABOUT AN ANIMAL THAT RANKED "FIRST AMONG THE WORKS OF GOD" (JOB 40:19), whose tail was so massive it swayed "like a cedar" (40:17). What kind of animal was it? It is called *behemot* in the Hebrew language and "behemoth" in English. But what exactly was this behemoth?

Many people believe that the behemoth of Job's day (roughly 4,000 years ago) was either a hippo or an elephant. Granted, these land animals are some of the largest on Earth today, and they do fit some of the description of behemoth. But neither the hippo nor the elephant "moves his tail like a cedar." A hippo has a little 6-8 inch "twig," not a stiff or large "cedar" tail like behemoth. And the elephant's tail isn't much more imposing than the hippo's.

So what could the behemoth have been? What creature with a mighty tail did God make that once inhabited the Earth with Job? What animal grew a tail 25-35 feet long that weighed thousands of pounds?

God's description of behemoth actually sounds more like one of the large plant-eating reptiles of the past (like *Diplodocus* or *Argentinosaurus*) than any other animal alive today. What other animal's tail could be sensibly described as "moving," "swaying," or "stiffening" **like a cedar**?

This dinosaur (or dinosaur-like creature) that roamed the Earth in Job's day is a reminder of God's greatness. The behemoth was strong and powerful (40:16), with bones "like beams of bronze" and "ribs like bars of iron" (40:18). "Look now at the behemoth which I made along with you" (Job 40:15) and consider how God's earthly creation declares His glory.

Painting by Lewis Lavoie

A Fire-Breathing Reptile?

Image by Lewis Lavoie

"His breath kindles coals, and a flame goes out of his mouth" (Job 40:21).

NO DOUBT YOU HAVE HEARD REPORTS

FROM WORLD HISTORY OF FIRE-BREATHING "DRAGONS." ALTHOUGH MANY OF THESE STORIES MAY HAVE BEEN EXAGGERATED (SIMILAR to the way people exaggerate the size of fish they catch or deer they kill), the idea of a fire-breathing animal should not be too hard to accept. Surely atheists, who mistakenly believe everything evolved from nothing and life popped out of non-life, would not think it would be impossible for a fire-breathing animal to evolve. What's more, creationists have no reason to think that an all-powerful, all-knowing Creator could not make such a creature. After all, God did create insects that light up, eels that can shock other animals without hurting themselves, and bombardier beetles that can expel powerful chemicals from their bodies at 212 degrees Fahrenheit (the boiling point of water).

Another even greater reason exists for believing in the one-time existence of a fire-breathing animal—God said that one existed in the days of Job. In chapter 41 of the book of Job, God described to the patriarch a real, terrifying, fire-breathing animal, saying:

> His sneezings flash forth light, and his eyes are like the eyelids of the morning. Out of his mouth go burning lights; sparks of fire shoot out. Smoke goes out of his nostrils, as from a boiling pot and burning rushes. His breath kindles coals, and a flame goes out of his mouth (vss. 18-21).

What is this amazing creature that God described in His conversation with Job? It is called "leviathan" (luh-VIE-uh-thun) in verse one of the chapter. But just what is a leviathan? Some suggest that leviathan is a crocodile. Others believe that it is a whale. However, the description of leviathan simply does not fit either of these two animals. In fact, the description of this creature does not fit that of any known animal present in the world today. Thus, it must be some type of extinct creature. But what kind?

God's description of leviathan is similar in every way with the descriptions we have of some of the dinosaur-like, water-living reptiles that roamed the Earth, not millions of years ago as some believe, but only a few thousand years ago when Job was alive.

The fact is, most people don't think that leviathan was a dinosaur-like reptile because they believe that dinosaurs and humans never lived together on the Earth at the same time. Yet the Bible says: "For in six days the Lord made the heavens and the earth, the sea, and **all** that is in them" (Exodus 20:11). Thus, if ever there was a creature like leviathan upon the Earth (and clearly God teaches there was), then it must have been created either on the fifth or sixth day of Creation (see Genesis 1:20-31).

Picture used with permission from Dr. Thomas Eisner

Bombardier Beetle

Firefly

3

BIRDS

E7 Did Not EVOLVE

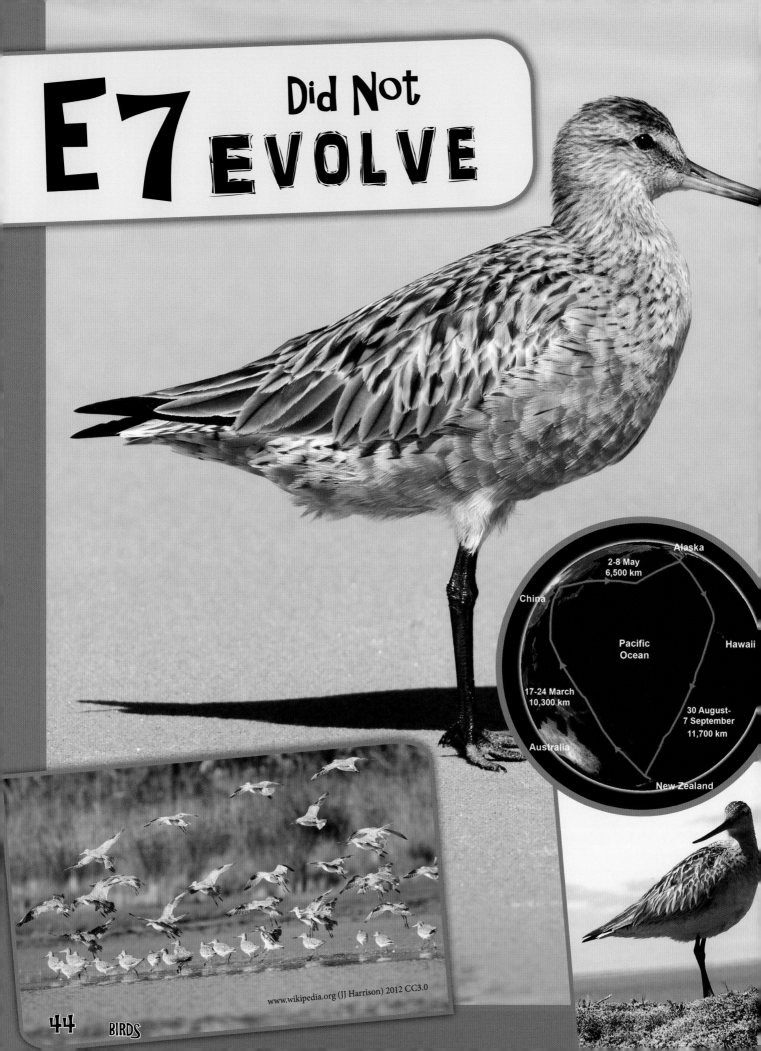

Alaska
2-8 May
6,500 km
China
Pacific Ocean
Hawaii
17-24 March
10,300 km
30 August-
7 September
11,700 km
Australia
New Zealand

www.wikipedia.org (JJ Harrison) 2012 CC3.0

IMAGINE A ROBOTIC BIRD

BUILT BY SCIENTISTS, WEIGHING LESS THAN ONE POUND AND ABLE TO FLY NON-stop more than 7,000 miles. Without ever stopping to oil its wings, tighten its screws, clean its gears, or recharge its lightweight batteries, this flying machine weighing less than a stapler could fly all the way from New York to Las Vegas and back. What's more, this robo-bird need not be controlled remotely, because it was programmed ahead of time to fly precisely from one place to another. With perfect precision, it lands in the intended spot.

Can you imagine such a flying machine? It would take thousands of hours, millions of dollars, and extremely intelligent scientists to design and build such an amazing robotic bird. No flying robot has ever accomplished such great feats. There is, however, a real bird that has.

In February 2007, scientists from the U.S. Geological Survey fitted 16 shorebirds, known as bar-tailed godwits, with satellite transmitters. One of the godwits named E7 made its way from New Zealand to Alaska over the following three months, flying more than 9,000 miles with one layover on the North Korea-China border. After nearly four months in Alaska, the godwit began its uninterrupted flight back to New Zealand. Amazingly, this little bird, which normally weighs less than one pound, flew **7,145 miles in nine days without stopping, averaging 34.8 miles per hour.** Without taking a break to eat, drink, or rest, the godwit flew the equivalent of a trip from New York to Las Vegas and back.

Equally impressive is the godwit's sense of direction. Every year, millions of humans travel to see the mountains of East Tennessee, the white, sandy beaches of Florida, and the giant Redwood trees of California. Can you imagine how difficult these journeys would be without the help

of maps, signs, satellites, or compasses? We simply could not go very far on Earth and expect to reach our intended destination without certain navigational aids. Amazingly, without help from a GPS or a compass, the godwit's 16,500-mile roundtrip journey ended exactly where it began.

Scientists have studied the flight of birds for decades and still cannot adequately explain our feathered friends' stamina and sense of direction. How can a person reasonably conclude that non-intelligence, plus time, plus chance equals a one-pound, bar-tailed godwit flying 7,145 miles in nine days without stopping for food, water, or rest?

The fact is, evolution cannot logically explain how a bird "soars, stretching his wings toward the south" (Job 39:26). Rather, "the stork in the sky knows her seasons; and the turtledove and the swift and the thrush observe the time of their migration" (Jeremiah 8:7, NASB), because all-knowing, all-powerful Jehovah is the Creator of them all.

www.wikipedia.org (Andreas Trepte, www.photonatur.de) 2012 CC2.5

Arctic Terns also Testify to GOD'S Greatness

Arctic terns fly thousands of miles in only a few weeks.

MIGRATION CHAMPION

AS THE NAME IMPLIES, ARCTIC TERNS

LIVE IN THE ARCTIC REGIONS OF THE EARTH. DURING THE SPRING, THEY BREED AND RAISE THEIR YOUNG IN SUCH PLACES AS CANADA, GREENLAND, and northern Russia. They feed on insects, worms, fish, and crustaceans. Then, in the fall of the year, they begin their migration south, to their Antarctic winter feeding grounds.

This journey is no walk in the park. Arctic terns fly thousands of miles in only a few weeks to reach their destination. One Arctic tern was tracked migrating from above the Arctic Circle in northern Russia all the way to Australia—a trip of 14,000 miles. Another Arctic tern (weighing only a few ounces) was tagged in Canada before it was old enough to fly. Just 90 days later, however, it was picked up in southern Africa—9,000 miles away.

Like the bar-tailed godwit, this migration champion owes its airborne abilities to Almighty God.

> One Arctic tern was tracked migrating from above the Arctic Circle in Northern Russia all the way to Australia—a trip of 14,000 miles.

Wondrous WOODPECKERS

Incredibly, woodpeckers can strike a hard surface 20 times per second and several thousand times a day without ever getting hurt. How forceful are woodpeckers' strikes? According to researchers, they are "equivalent to **1,000 times** the force of gravity," or "**more than 250 times** the force to which an astronaut is subjected in a rocket during liftoff." So powerful are woodpeckers' strikes that some scientists believe that they close their eyes in between each peck—not to keep chips of wood from getting in their eyes—but to keep their eyeballs from popping out of their sockets as they strike the tree with such tremendous force.

How can woodpeckers survive such a head banging? How do their craniums not crack and brains not burst? First, woodpeckers have very strong, extra thick skulls, which can take a pounding without cracking. Second, and perhaps more important, woodpeckers have special shock absorbers that are better than anything man has ever made—better than the best car bumper, and better than any shock-absorbing football helmet. In the perfect place (right in-between the bird's beak and skull),

HAVE YOU EVER
HAD A HEAD INJURY? PERHAPS YOU HAVE BUMPED HEADS WITH SOMEONE and developed a knot on your forehead. Maybe you have tripped over a curb, hit your head on the pavement, and suffered a concussion (brain injury). I once saw a boy run full-speed into a large tree, accidentally striking it with his head. Talk about a painful experience! Though the human body is perfectly designed for God's purposes in creating it, God did not create humans in the same way that He designed woodpeckers. If a human were to strike a tree with the force and regularity that a woodpecker knocks against it, he would soon die. Woodpeckers, however, keep on keeping on.

Arctic Woodpeckers drill into trees for at least three reasons: (1) to find insects to eat; (2) to carve out a hole in which to live; and (3) to communicate with other woodpeckers.

The woodpecker's beak is so strong it can remain perfectly straight and functional for more than 10 years and through more than 10 million pecks against a tree. It never has to be replaced or sharpened.

God created the perfect sponge-like tissue to absorb the perpetual pounding that this bird puts itself through on a daily basis.

Once woodpeckers carve a hole into a tree, how do they get to the insects that may still be four or five inches away? If their tongues were short like most birds, much of the pecking woodpeckers do would be rather useless, because they would not be able to reach the insects. But God knew what woodpeckers needed. He gave them elongated tongues, which they can roll up and store deep in their skulls when not extended. Some woodpeckers have tongues that are five inches long (or three times the length of their beaks). What's more, their tongues are specially designed with rear-facing barbs and a sticky substance that help draw insects out of the tree and back to the woodpeckers.

1. Why did woodpeckers ever start banging their beaks on trees for food when they could simply gather food on the ground like most other birds?

2. How did the first woodpecker not kill itself the first time it began beating its beak against a tree?

3. How did the first woodpecker know to close its eyes every time it struck a tree?

4. When did the woodpecker get the special, shock-absorbing cushion between its beak and skull?

5. If this special cushion took millions of years to evolve, what did woodpeckers do in the meantime?

6. From where did woodpeckers get their sticky, barbed, elongated tongues that are perfectly designed for woodpeckers to stick into trees?

7. Why is the tongue of woodpeckers so different from ordinary birds?

8. How did woodpeckers know that they could generate more force per peck if they had stiff tail feathers as well as two toes in the front and two toes in the back to anchor their positions to trees?

9. Who taught woodpeckers that they could chisel trees in search of food?

10. Who taught them to communicate with each other by banging their bills against trees?

11. Who taught them to drill holes into trees for shelter?

12. Why are other birds not evolving these amazing abilities, like the woodpecker supposedly did?

The fact is, the idea that the wondrous woodpecker could evolve is absurd. This amazing bird did not have to knock itself silly for millions of years in hopes of one day getting everything it needed to do what it does. On day five of Creation (Genesis 1:20-23), Almighty God specially designed the woodpecker with a strong bill, a thick skull, a long tongue, and the best shock absorber in the world.

Unlike most birds, woodpeckers have two toes that point forward and two toes that point backward. This perfect design helps keep woodpeckers secure against trees as they drill their holes.

? HAVE YOU CONSIDERED...?

FEATHERED TAILS TESTIFY TO THE TRUTH OF CREATION

God designed birds with some of the most beautiful and practical tails in the animal kingdom. Birds use their feathered tails to do all sorts of things. Similar to a rudder on the tail of an airplane, a bird's tail can function like a rudder to help steer it while in flight. The surface area of the tail can also help produce lift while in the air. When perched, a bird uses its tail feathers to provide balance. Birds can also use their tails to communicate to each other. A wagging or flipping tail can indicate happiness, while tail fanning may be a bird's way of showing its strength or anger.

God did not have to "try out" tails on birds to see if they would be helpful. He knew they would be helpful all along. In His infinite wisdom, He created our feathered, flying friends on the fifth day of Creation (Genesis 1:20-23) with a variety of marvelous, well-designed tails.

Peacocks have some of the largest and most colorful tail feathers of any bird. They can grow more than four feet in length.

A hawk spreads its tail feathers out to soar and folds them together when swooping down like a dart to attack its prey.

The long, stiff tail feathers of woodpeckers are perfectly designed to help provide support while woodpeckers drill into trees in search of insects.

The Master's Magnificent Mallee Fowl

HOW DO

YOU FIND OUT EXACTLY HOW HOT or cold it is outside? Do you take a deep breath? Do you put your finger high in the air? Or do you perhaps put your nose to the ground? Of course not. When you want to know the exact temperature you simply go check a thermometer. But how amazing would it be to identify the exact temperature simply by putting your nose to the ground? One animal that lives in Australia can do exactly that.

The mallee fowl is a chicken-sized bird that lives in the mallee forests of southern Australia. (Mallee is a type of low-growing eucalyptus plant.) Prior to the mallee fowl hen laying her eggs, the male spends several weeks or months preparing a special mound in which the eggs will incubate. The male first digs a hole about three feet deep and 10-15 feet in diameter. Next, the male begins to construct the mound over the hole using leaves, twigs, dirt, and sand. Eventually the mound will reach a height of about five feet.

The hen will then lay anywhere from 20-35 eggs in a dug-out section of the mound over a period of

BELOW IS AN IMAGE OF A MALLEE FOWL MOUND. THESE MOUNDS VARY IN SIZE, BUT ARE GENERALLY ABOUT 10-15 FEET WIDE AND 3-5 FEET HIGH.

several weeks. The male keeps a close watch over the eggs and mound, ensuring that everything stays very near 92°F. How does he do this? He simply sticks his beak and tongue into the mound. The bird can tell if the temperature is too high or too low. The mallee might scrape some of the mound away to cool the eggs, or it might build up the mound even more in order to raise the temperature.

Thermometers were developed and designed by highly intelligent men over several centuries. But what about the mallee fowl's built-in thermometer? Who designed it? And how is the mallee fowl able to construct a massive nest and manage it so capably? Evolutionists would have us believe that time and chance gave the mallee fowl all of these abilities. Common sense, however, demands a better explanation: Complex design demands a designer. Mallee fowl, along with all birds, were designed by God.

HOW AMAZING WOULD IT BE TO IDENTIFY THE EXACT TEMPERATURE SIMPLY BY PUTTING YOUR NOSE TO THE GROUND?

FISH
...and Other
Sea Creatures

4

The COELACANTH: Misunderstood or Missing Link?

www.wikipedia.org (Afernand74) 2012 CC3.0

www.wikipedia.org (Haplochromis) 2012 CC3.0

FOR DECADES,

EVOLUTIONISTS TAUGHT THAT COELACANTHS (SEE-LUH-KANTHS) became extinct about the same time dinosaurs did (supposedly 65 million years ago). People were told that these fish gradually developed legs and began to live on Earth, and sometime later became extinct. Evolutionists thought that these fish were the "missing link" between water and land animals. Similar to the ape-like creatures that supposedly evolved into humans, these fish were said to have evolved into land animals millions of years ago. In fact, evolutionary scientists used the coelacanth as a part of their "index fossil" system, meaning

Picture compliments of Mark Erdmann

Painting by Lewis Lavoie

(an island off the eastern coast of Africa). The fishermen who netted the fish, having no idea of its proper name, called it "the great sea lizard" because its pectoral fins looked more like little legs. Once scientists examined this strange creature, however, they confirmed what was formerly thought to be impossible—a coelacanth had been caught in modern times!

Since 1938, over 100 additional coelacanths have been caught. In 1952 they were seen swimming near the Comoro Islands in the Indian Ocean. Another population was found in 1998 off the coast of Indonesia. Surprisingly, local Indonesian fishermen were quite familiar with this fish, as they had been catching them for years—even though scientists were totally unaware they lived in that region.

Modern-day coelacanths look exactly like their fossil counterparts (which are mistakenly dated as being millions of years old). The fact that these modern creatures have stayed the same as their fossilized ancestors is no surprise to Christians. The Bible teaches that animals reproduce "after their kind" (Genesis 1:21, 24), and the fossil record proves that this is exactly what has happened. Fish never gradually developed over millions of years into land animals, any more than ape-like creatures ever developed into humans. Coelacanths are still coelacanths, and apes are still apes.

Did You Know?

The "living fossil" known as the coelacanth is a thorn in the side of evolutionists. It makes a mockery of evolutionary dating methods, provides further proof that "missing links" are myths, and exposes evolutionists' "facts" for what they really are—**unproven assumptions**.

that any rocks that contained coelacanth fossils were considered to be at least 65 million years old (with other fossils in those rocks assumed to be at least that old as well).

Until 1938, evolutionists believed that humans and coelacanths could not possibly have lived at the same time. These creatures were known only from the fossils that these same evolutionists claimed were many millions of years old. But then, on December 24, 1938, the scientific world was rocked when an unidentified fish five feet long and over 100 pounds was brought to shore in South Africa. It was caught in the Indian Ocean near Madagascar

Believed to be extinct, a coelacanth was caught in 1938 off the coast of South Africa.

POLYPTERUS' PROTECTIVE COVERING POINTS to GOD

www.wikipedia.org (Conscious) 2012 CC3.0

OPERATING ON FUNDING

RECEIVED FROM THE U.S. ARMY, SCIENTISTS FROM THE MASSACHUSETTS INSTITUTE OF Technology (MIT) are developing better body armor for soldiers. Surprisingly, the inspiration for their work comes from a foot-long African fish known as *Polypterus senegalus*.

The fish's "armor" is able to protect it from its own species, as well as from other carnivores (meat-eating animals). According to researchers, the overlapping protective scales of *Polypterus senegalus* "first dissipate the energy of a strike, then protect against any penetrations to the soft tissues below and finally limit any damage to the shield to the immediate area surrounding the assault." What makes the fish's armor so effective? Aside from its four layers of overlapping scales, scientists believe the dermal scales' complex materials (including bone and dentine), as well as the arrangement and thickness of the different layers of scales, all contribute to the armor's strength and ability to protect the animal. One scientist stated: "Such fundamental knowledge holds great potential for the development of improved biologically inspired structural materials."

Brilliant scientists in the 21st century are spending an untold amount of time, energy, and money studying the scale structure of a fish, in hopes of designing new and improved armor applications for U.S. soldiers and military vehicles. Scientists admit that the "design" of the overlapping scale layers is "fascinating" and "complex." Yet, at the same time, atheistic evolutionists tell us that this fish, which is inspiring state-of-the-art human armor systems, had no designer. But design demands a designer. An effect (especially one of this magnitude) demands an adequate cause. In truth, blind chance, plus non-intelligence, plus random mutations, plus eons of time did not cause *Polypterus senegalus*. Only an intelligent Designer could make such an awe-inspiring creature. As the psalmist wrote: "This great and wide sea, in which are innumerable teeming things, living things both small and great. O Lord, how manifold are Your works! In wisdom You have made them all" (Psalm 104:25,24).

www.wikipedia.org (Stan Shebs) 2012 CC3.0

The CREATOR'S CAVE FISH

DID YOU KNOW THAT SOME ANIMALS LIVE THEIR ENTIRE LIVES IN CAVES—WITHOUT EVER LEAVING?

Various cave fish spend their entire lives in caves in complete darkness. Because food is scarce in caves, these fish tend to be only four or five inches long. With no need for camouflage or protection from the Sun, cave fish have no pigmentation—their skin is either stark white or transparent. Some, like the ones located in Mammoth Cave of Kentucky, are completely blind. Other cave fish have no eyes at all. You might wonder how these sightless fish swim without bumping into everything. And how do they hunt for food? Cave fish have highly sensitive barbels (whisker-like organs similar to those found on catfish) arranged over the head and body. These sensory organs allow the fish to feel what it cannot see.

They make it possible for the fish to hunt for food and to detect nearby predators.

Some evolutionists claim that because these fish have no eyesight and are well adapted to living in caves, then evolution must be true. Scientists today believe that these fish are the offspring of fish that once had eyes. But losing a feature doesn't help prove the theory of evolution. Plus, cave fish are still fish. They have not evolved from or into a frog, a snake, or any other animal. The only difference between cave fish and other fish is that they have adapted to their environment in a special way. Just because a fish's eyes no longer function does not mean that the fish somehow "evolved" in the past, or will do so in the future. Fish, as well as all animals, certainly can adapt to their environments, but there is no evidence that any kind of animal ever evolved into a different kind of creature. The fact is, the Creator's cave fish, whether blind or eyeless, whether white or transparent, have always been and always will be… just fish.

Cave fish have highly sensitive barbels.

SUPER SEAHORSES

THE SEAHORSE IS ONE

OF THE MOST CURIOUS-LOOKING ANIMALS ON THE PLANET. THOUGH IT HAS A head like a horse, eyes like a lizard, a tail like an opossum, and can swim like a submarine, the seahorse is considered a fish. Scientists put seahorses in the pipefish/sea dragon family and refer to it as *Hippocampus*, a name derived from two Greek words: *hippo*, meaning "horse," and *campus*, meaning "sea creature."

Submarine-Swimming Sensations

Most fish swim horizontally by moving their bodies back and forth, from side to side, somewhat like a snake wriggles. Seahorses, on the other hand, are upright and swim vertically—like a submarine that can go up and down. How do they accomplish such a feat? A seahorse has one fin on its back and one on each side of its neck that help to propel it. But what helps maintain its balance as it goes up and down in the water is the gas within its swim bladder. Like a well-designed submarine that manipulates gas in order to submerge and resurface while remaining parallel to the water, the seahorse can alternate the amount of gas in its bladder to do the same. The life of the seahorse is dependent on a perfectly designed bladder. With a damaged bladder (or without a bladder altogether) a seahorse would sink to the ocean floor and die. One wonders how evolutionists can explain the evolution of the swim bladder if seahorses have always needed them

to survive. If they have always needed them, then they must have always had them, else there would be no seahorses. But there are seahorses—and small though they be, they stand as powerful witnesses for the Creator.

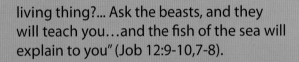
Male seahorses actually get pregnant, carry the babies, and give birth.

Mr. Mom Defies Evolution

Female dogs have puppies. Female cats have kittens. Female horses (called mares) have baby horses (called foals). Women, not men, become pregnant, and carry and deliver babies. With seahorses, however, things are different. Seahorses are the only known animals in which the males actually get pregnant, carry the babies, and give birth.

God designed the male seahorse with a special kangaroo-like pouch near its belly. At just the right time during the courtship, the female seahorse deposits hundreds of eggs into the pouch of the male, where he fertilizes them. For the next few weeks, the male seahorse carries the unborn seahorses, before squirting the fully formed babies out of the pouch.

If nothing like this process is known in the animal kingdom, why would anyone think that evolution can logically explain it? How do undirected time and chance stumble across a different and better way for a particular kind of fish to have babies? Did the first male seahorse to give birth simply have an irritable wife who refused to have babies unless he carried and birthed them? Suffice it to say, seahorses are as baffling to the theory of evolution as duck-billed platypuses. These unusual animals cry out for a creative Creator, Who cannot be contained in the naturalistic box of evolution. As the patriarch Job asked, "Who…does not know that the hand of the Lord has done this, in whose hand is the life of every

living thing?... Ask the beasts, and they will teach you…and the fish of the sea will explain to you" (Job 12:9-10,7-8).

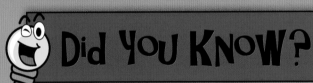

Did You Know?

The Perfectly Designed Prehensile Tail

The tail of a seahorse is wonderfully designed. As with the opossum and certain monkeys, God gave the seahorse a prehensile (pre-HEN-sul) tail. A prehensile tail is one that can wrap around and hold things. Seahorses use their tails to wrap around seaweed and anchor themselves so that fast-moving water currents do not carry the rather slow-moving seahorses far away from their homes.

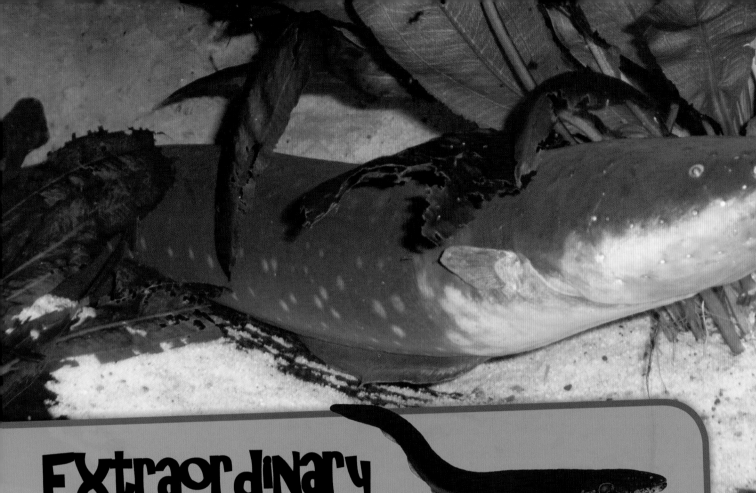

Extraordinary ELECTRIC EELS

UNLiKe MOSt FiSH, electric eeLS SWiM to the SurFace to breathe air.

ELECTRIC EELS ARE PUZZLING TO A LOT OF PEOPLE. THEIR SIX-FOOT-LONG, TUBULAR,

scaleless bodies look and move more like snakes than fish. But, like seahorses, electric eels are classified by scientists as fish. Adding to the confusion, however, is that scientists do not classify electric eels as eels, but knifefish.

So how do electric eels produce electric charges? It's all in the design of the animal. God made this curious creature with three pairs of organs (six in all), which make up nearly its entire tail region—about 80% of its body. These organs are made up of about 6,000 electro-plaques (i-LEK-tro-plaks). Electro-

www.wikipedia.org (Steven G. Johnson) 2012 CC3.0

www.wikipedia.org (Steven G. Johnson) 2012 CC3.0

plaques are muscles arranged like batteries. These muscles do not contract like normal muscles. Instead, they give off electrical charges. At will, an electric eel can send signals from its brain, through various nerves, to its battery-like muscles. What's more, this divinely designed creature can choose to produce a small current of electricity, or it can carry out a shock of up to 600 volts—enough to stun a horse.

Electric eels use this electrical current for a variety of reasons. First, as you would guess, they use this ability for self-defense purposes. Who wants to mess with a fish that can electrocute you? Second, they use it in order to stun or kill their prey. Third, they use it to communicate with other electric eels. And finally, since they normally live in the slow moving, murky rivers and streams of South America, electric eels can set their "batteries" on low and create an electromagnetic field that helps them navigate. They can detect underwater objects, including prey and predators.

Did You Know?

How could evolutionary theory ever adequately explain a creature as extraordinary as the electric eel?

- How did the first electric eel evolve from a non-electric eel?

- How did all of the "batteries" of the first electric eel get put in precisely the right place in order to produce electricity after receiving signals from the animal's brain by way of special nerves?

- How can evolutionists logically explain the electric eel's ability to not shock itself whenever it produces electric charges?

- How would it have known it needed to evolve a special layer of fat around its body in order to protect itself from electric currents that it had never yet produced?

- And if the animal had not yet produced its special "insulation," how would it have survived continued electrocutions without it?

The only explanation that logically explains the first electric eel is God. On day five of Creation, He specially designed "every living thing that moves, with which the waters abounded" (Genesis 1:21), including the extraordinary electric eel.

FISH...AND OTHER SEA CREATURES

CUTTLEFISH: The Creator's King of Camouflage

ITS EYES ARE LIKE

SOMETHING FROM A BATMAN MOVIE. ITS FEEDING TENTACLES SHOOT OUT OF ITS mouth like a birthday party blower. Its blood is bluish green, and its "ink" is black. (Cuttlefish, like octopuses and squid, can eject a cloud of black ink into the water, which can distract attackers long enough for them to escape.) Scientists believe that these amazing animals have a complicated system of communicating with each other, including the use of 40 different body patterns.

Making the cuttle**fish** even stranger is the fact that it is not even a fish, but a mollusk. (Who named this animal, anyway?) Cuttlefish have an internal shell called a cuttlebone, so scientists put them into the shell (mollusk) group.

Perhaps the most amazing feature of cuttlefish is their ability to blend in to their surroundings. Cuttlefish have been said to have "the world's best camouflage skills." First, cuttlefish can change the texture of their skin to mimic the shape of certain rocks or corals. Second, these mollusks can move their entire bodies into a variety of positions. For example, while swimming

next to large seaweed, cuttlefish can mimic the grass's motion by positioning and waving their eight arms in a similar way that the seaweed sways in the water. This makes it very difficult for both attackers and possible prey to know the precise location of a cuttlefish.

In a recent study, scientists placed horizontal or vertical stripes on the walls of cuttlefish tanks. How did the cuttlefish react? These animals spread their bodies out horizontally when in the horizontally lined tanks (where lines went from side to side), and they raised at least one arm vertically when in the vertically lined tanks (where lines went up and down). What amazing mimicking ability!

Finally, what must annoy predators more than anything is the cuttlefish's ability to change color—and to do it so quickly. A cuttlefish can change the color of its entire body in the blink of an eye. If this mollusk wants to change to red, it sends signals from its brain to its pigment (or color) sacs to change to red. Cuttlefish can hide from other sea life by changing to the color of sand or seaweed. It can also appear as a strobe light, blinking "on and off" very quickly, possibly to confuse predators.

Cuttlefish are remarkable creatures. If evolution is true, how did the cuttlefish evolve pigment sacs that have the ability to produce a variety of colors at will? How do cuttlefish know they have changed to a particular color if they cannot see themselves? Also, if, as scientists believe, this animal is color-blind, how does it always choose the color most helpful (like changing to the color of sand when on the ocean floor)? Scientists do not have a "natural" answer for these questions. Why? Because the cuttlefish was created by a **supernatural** Creator. God alone is the cause of the cuttlefish.

? HAVE YOU CONSIDERED....?

ROBOLOBSTERS BY DESIGN

Why would scientists spend many thousands of dollars building a 7-pound, 24-inch lobster-like robot? Why did *TIME* Magazine once recognize RoboLobster as one of the "Coolest Inventions"? We normally think of lobsters as a kind of food to eat at our favorite seafood restaurant, and not the inspiration for some grand invention.

Scientists are mimicking lobsters because the U.S. Navy is in need of a better way to hunt for deadly explosives (called mines) on the ocean floor. The ocean can be a very difficult place to look for mines because of the rush of waves and the difficulty of seeing clearly through the water. Now scientists have devised a new way. Well, actually, they have copied the appearance and abilities of real lobsters.

Lobsters move with tremendous ease, both over land and through turbulent waters. They can easily adjust their position in the rough waters of the ocean. They are able to contract their tails quickly in order to scoot away from danger. And they can effectively walk along sand and rocks preying on starfish, sea urchins, and clams. RoboLobster was built to imitate the movement of the real lobster. Scientists believe that RoboLobster will be able to search for mines along the coastlines by mimicking the motions of real lobsters.

Imagine seeing RoboLobster crawling in the shallow waters off of a beach. Its eight super-strong plastic legs work just right to move it in any direction. Its antennae sense obstacles to avoid or destroy. Its claws and tail stabilize it in rough waters. After observing it for a short period of time, you would surely conclude that this robot is the product of intelligent design.

Now imagine seeing a **real** lobster scurrying along the same ocean floor. You recognize that its body is designed perfectly for the actions it performs. You observe its claws, legs, eyes, antennae, and tail. You watch how easily it moves around, automatically adjusting its body in the turbulent waters in order to stay in just the right position to rest or search for food.

To what do we owe the real, living lobster? Evolutionists say it is the result of mindless time and chance. However, common sense and the Bible say otherwise. Design demands a Designer. "For every house is built by someone, but He who built all things is God" (Hebrews 3:4).

Photo of RoboLobster. (U.S. Navy photograph by John F. Williams - 3/2/2006)

5 insects

BEETLES

Click Beetle

There are more than 350,000 different species of beetles in the world.

THERE ARE MORE SPECIES OF BEETLES

IN THE WORLD THAN ANY OTHER KIND OF INSECT. MORE THAN 350,000 DIFFERENT SPECIES ARE ESTIMATED, WITH MORE BEING DISCOVERED each year. Beetles vary in size and shape. Some have a long and narrow "neck," like the giraffe weevil. Others, like the ladybug, are short and round. Despite their differences in size, beetles have one feature in common—a pair of hard front wings that cover the back wings like a case. These rigid wing covers prevent the back wings from being damaged by other animals.

Giraffe Weevil

Dung Beetles—Having just formed a ball of dung from animal feces, these beetles are rolling it into a hiding place. Eventually, they will lay eggs on the ball. Then, when the baby beetles (called larvae) hatch, they will feed on the feces. How amazing is it that the Creator made bugs that would even devour dung?

Dung Beetles

Rhinoceros Beetle

Rhinoceros Beetle—This beetle gets its name from the well-designed horn-like structures on the thorax, the area just behind the head. These horns are sometimes used when struggling with other insects.

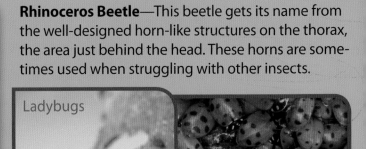
Ladybugs

Ladybugs—These cute little beetles are excellent insects to have around. They feed on other insects that attack trees, shrubs, and vegetable crops.

Weevil

Scientists estimate that four out of every ten species of insects are beetles, including click beetles, dung beetles, Rhinoceros beetles, ladybugs, and boll weevils. In one sense, beetles are common creatures. That is, they are commonly **seen** creatures. But don't think of them as unremarkable animals: beetles do some exceptional things that testify to a grand Designer. Consider two examples: the bombardier beetle and the lightning bug.

The BOMBARDIER BEETLE:
A BOMBSHELL FOR EVOLUTIONISTS

Picture used with permission from Dr. Thomas Eisner

WHAT IS SO SPECIAL ABOUT THIS LITTLE BUG? OF ALL

the things to consider in life, why would a one-half-inch-long, average-looking beetle be worthy of our consideration? Because this beetle is a ticking time bomb.

No, the bombardier beetle does not have explosives tied to its back. It doesn't carry around a miniature stick of dynamite. Nor are its insides full of nitroglycerin (nie-truh-GLIS-er-in)—the explosive liquid present in dynamite and other explosives. What does the bombardier beetle possess that makes it so unique? This little bug has tiny glands inside its body that hold two harmless chemicals known as hydroquinones (hi-dro-KWI-nons) and (the more familiar) hydrogen peroxide. The bombardier beetle secretes these chemicals into a kind of "holding area" or "storage tank." Then, if the beetle senses danger and is agitated by an attacker, it quickly moves the chemicals from its storage tank into yet another chamber, which could be called the "explosion chamber." In this compartment, the beetle secretes special catalyst enzymes into the once-harmless chemical mixture, making a toxic spray that reaches 212 degrees Fahrenheit (or 100 degrees Celsius)—the temperature at which water boils.

Amazingly, the beetle doesn't blow up. It doesn't develop a high fever and die. The noxious spray doesn't eat through the chamber walls and kill the beetle. No, the beetle sizes up its attacker and quickly rotates two rear nozzles at the end of the explosion chamber so that they point in the direction of the attacker. The bombardier beetle then fires the boiling-hot mixture toward the enemy with pinpoint-accuracy in a high-speed, machine-gun-like fashion—at about 500 "rounds" (pulses) of toxic spray per second.

Evolutionists allege that this amazing insect is the product of millions of years of evolution. Can you imagine the evolution of a bombardier beetle? If this theory were true, then there had to have been a time when the bombardier beetle did not produce a toxic spray. There had to have been a time when it didn't store a 212-degree-mixture. There had to have been a time when it had never shot anything out of its back end as hot as boiling water. If so, what would have happened the first time the beetle evolved the ability to mix a boiling-hot solution, without already having a storage tank in place that could withstand such temperatures? What would have happened the first time this beetle ever blew a "bomb" out its backend? Why did the beetle not blow up the first time it ever created a "bomb"? The answer: because the bombardier beetle did not evolve by time and chance, and unintelligent, natural processes over millions of years. Common sense calls for a Creator Who made this insect with all of its necessary parts in place at the same time—at Creation. The amazing defense mechanism of the bombardier beetle declares the glory of God and defies the theory of evolution.

The CREATOR'S COOL LIGHT: LIGHTNING BUGS

HAVE YOU EVER TRIED TO

UNSCREW A LIGHT BULB FROM A LAMP THAT HAS BEEN ON FOR 10 OR 15 MINUTES? I DON'T RECOMmend that you attempt this, but if you have, you know that standard light bulbs get very hot, very quickly—and remain hot the whole time they are on. The average bulb lights up when the tiny filament inside is heated by the electricity that passes through it. Unfortunately, heat and light bulbs go hand in hand. About 95% of the energy produced by a light bulb is lost in the form of heat. For this reason, scientists have looked for new ways to produce cheaper and safer forms of light.

One "new" form of light involves chemical reactions without the addition of heat. You probably have seen this kind of light in the form of glow sticks (or light sticks). These tubes of light have become very popular in recent years. People use them for all sorts of things. Once when I

For years scientists have studied fireflies in hopes of learning how they produce "cold light."

was staying at a hotel and the electricity was off for a few hours, I used these sticks to see where I was going. People like them so much because they produce light without heat. (And they look pretty cool, too!)

People seem to overlook the fact that this technology is not new. Man did not invent this kind of light. It has actually been here since the Creation when God made lightning bugs. These insects (also called fireflies) are little beetles that carry their own "flashlights." These insects have special chemicals called luciferin (lew-SI-fer-in) and luciferase (lew-SI-fer-ace), which they combine with oxygen to form a bright, heatless light. This process is called bioluminescence (by-oh-LOO-meh-NESS-sense)—the emission of light from living organisms.

For years scientists have studied fireflies in hopes of learning how they produce "cold light." And they have been somewhat successful. But scientists confess that light from fireflies (and certain other bioluminescent creatures) is still many times more efficient than what they can produce in laboratories.

The more scientists learn about the firefly, the more amazed they are at its complexity. Sadly, many of these same scientists believe that the firefly simply evolved over millions of years by time, chance, and random mutations. They dismiss both its obvious design and the Great Designer Who created it.

ROBOTIC FLIES and their Superior COUNTERPART

WHO MADE THE OFTEN IMITATED, BUT NEVER DUPLICATED, LIVING FLY?

FOR SEVERAL YEARS A TEAM OF SCIENTISTS
FROM HARVARD UNIVERSITY HAS STUDIED FLIES, ATTEMPTING TO BUILD A LIFE-SIZE, FLYING ROBOT THAT CAN MIMIC THE FLIGHT OF

living flies. The government is hopeful that robotic flies might one day be used as spies in secret missions, as well as to detect toxic chemicals used by terrorists. In 2007, it was announced that the "robotic fly has taken flight." One scientist called this robotic flying insect "a major breakthrough."

What do brilliant scientists have to show for over seven years of research? What was the "major breakthrough"? Why are scientists so excited? Because the life-size robotic fly…**took off**. It could not maneuver in the air. It was unable to be controlled. It could not avoid obstacles. It could not slow down and land on a specific target. It did not have its own power source (and even if it did, it would not have provided more than five minutes of power for flying). According to scientists, the robotic fly was "limited by a tether (string or rope) that keeps it moving in a straight, upward direction." Yet, since "a lot of people thought it would never be able to take off," such a feat is considered remarkable.

Admittedly, scientists have done a splendid job building a life-size robotic fly that can move upward on a tether by flapping its man-made wings. It takes extremely intelligent individuals to make a tiny robot that resembles and mimics (to some degree) living flies. Yet, some of these same scientists believe that real flies, which admittedly have "puzzled scientists and bedazzled engineers" with their "magical," "intricate maneuvers," are merely "nature made," rather than "God made." That is, flies supposedly are the result of evolution rather than creation. Such a thought defies common sense!

Were researchers to leave hundreds of tiny parts lying around in a lab for 100 years (or one billion years!), no reasonable person would conclude that, eventually, time and chance would assemble a robotic fly, much less one that moves as well as a real fly. It took several clever, hardworking scientists more than seven years just to make a robotic fly lift off the ground.

Who made the often imitated, but never duplicated, living fly that far surpasses the abilities of any robotic fly? Who designed the fly's sesame-seed size brain and its complicated flight dynamics that scientists have been unable to fully understand even after several years of study? God, not nature, makes the world's best fliers.

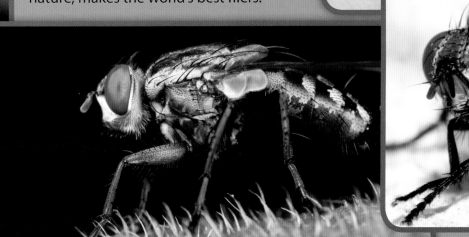

The Design of the Dragonfly

For dragonflies to be "marvels of flight engineering," logic demands that they had to be engineered...by someone.

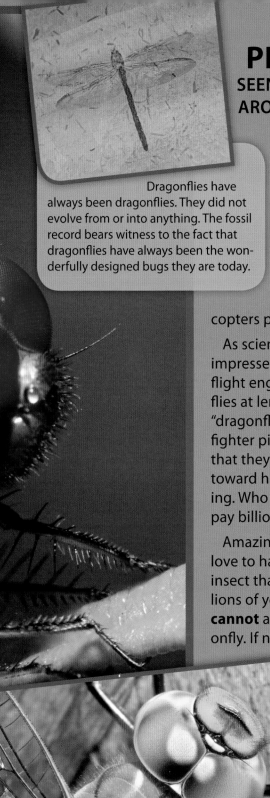

PERHAPS YOU HAVE
SEEN THE AMAZING DRAGONFLY AROUND PONDS, LAKES, AND RIVERS

and noticed how its ability to fly is second to none. Not only can dragonflies dash forward at speeds of nearly 40 miles per hour, but they can also use their four wings to fly backwards, straight up, and straight down. God designed the dragonfly so well that when humans began making helicopters in the mid 1900s, they looked to this insect for inspiration. In fact, one of the very first helicopters produced was named Dragonfly.

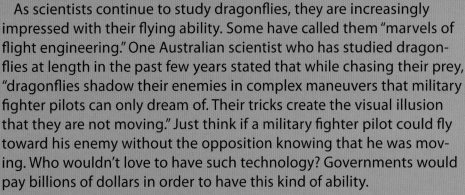

Dragonflies have always been dragonflies. They did not evolve from or into anything. The fossil record bears witness to the fact that dragonflies have always been the wonderfully designed bugs they are today.

As scientists continue to study dragonflies, they are increasingly impressed with their flying ability. Some have called them "marvels of flight engineering." One Australian scientist who has studied dragonflies at length in the past few years stated that while chasing their prey, "dragonflies shadow their enemies in complex maneuvers that military fighter pilots can only dream of. Their tricks create the visual illusion that they are not moving." Just think if a military fighter pilot could fly toward his enemy without the opposition knowing that he was moving. Who wouldn't love to have such technology? Governments would pay billions of dollars in order to have this kind of ability.

Amazingly, the information that scientists and governments would love to have is stored in the tiny brain and body of a dragonfly—an insect that evolutionists believe evolved by random processes millions of years ago. The truth is, however, time and chance **do not** and **cannot** account for the amazing design found in insects like the dragonfly. If no one considers the helicopter as the product of time and chance, why would anyone believe that the animal which scientists have tried to imitate evolved?

For dragonflies to be "marvels of flight engineering," logic demands that they had to be **engineered...by someone**. That Someone is God—the master Engineer and Designer of the fast, floating, mesmerizing dragonfly.

METAMORPHOSIS AND THE MAKER

Robots that can change into cars, trucks, planes, or motorcycles have entertained young people for several years. Young people have played with Transformers®, read stories about them in magazines, and even watched them come to life on TV and in the movies. Even some adults enjoy converting their children's Transformers® from one thing to another.

As exciting as converting toy Transformers® can be, a more amazing transformation process can be seen in the animal world. God designed some animals—certain insects, for instance—to go through major physical changes over the course of their lives. They do not evolve into other kinds of creatures, but undergo a process of major changes that allow them to develop properly. We call this process metamorphosis (meh-tuh-MOR-fuh-sis).

The first stage of metamorphosis is the egg stage. Insects (like the housefly) lay eggs, wherein embryos form. The embryos remain in the eggs anywhere from one day to one month.

When the creature exits the egg, it is known as a larva. Caterpillars are the larvae of butterflies and moths. Maggots are the larvae of flies. ("Larvae" is plural for larva.) Although with most insects this stage lasts only a few days or weeks, some cicadas remain underground in the larval stage for 17 years.

Next is the pupal stage. Not all creatures that undergo metamorphosis go through this stage (cockroaches, for example, do not). Insects like flies, moths, and butterflies, however, form pupae. ("Pupae" is plural for pupa.) When a moth caterpillar forms a cocoon, it is in the pupal stage. The insect undergoes major changes during this time. For example, this is when caterpillars develop their wings and become moths or butterflies. The pupal stage may last for days or weeks.

When an insect at the end of the pupal stage emerges from its case, a fully developed creature is seen. It is now an adult and will remain in this stage until it dies, which for many insects is not very long.

Metamorphosis is an incredible process. Like toy Transformers® that had to have been designed by intelligent toymakers, the much more sophisticated living animals that metamorphose must have been designed by an intelligent Designer.

Yahweh, Yucca Moths,
and a Young Creation

The flowers of yucca plants can only be pollinated by yucca moths.

A SYMBIOTIC RELATIONSHIP IS ONE

THAT IS MUTUALLY HELPFUL OR DEPENDENT. IN FOOTBALL, FOR EXAMPLE, A QUARTERBACK IS HELPED BY HAVING GOOD RECEIVERS, and receivers are helped by having a good quarterback. They depend on each other to succeed. When people think of symbiotic relationships, they often think about animals helping other animals. But it is also the case that many times animals assist plants, while plants, in return, help animals. Take, for instance, the yucca moth and the yucca plant created by Yahweh (the Hebrew word for Jehovah).

The pollination of yucca plants is different from all other plants. The flowers of yucca plants can **only** be pollinated by yucca moths. When a female yucca moth collects pollen from the yucca flower, she then bores holes and lays eggs in the base of the female part of the flower. Afterwards, the moth flies to the top of the flower and crawls onto the stigma, where it unloads the flower's pollen in order for pollination to occur.

Soon, the yucca flower will be able to produce seeds. In the meantime, the yucca moth eggs will have hatched. The moth caterpillars survive by eating some of the seeds of the yucca plant, which is all they eat—yucca seeds and yucca seeds only. But the caterpillars do not eat **all** of the seeds. Many seeds are left to fall to the ground to become new yucca plants.

Have you ever thought about how yucca moths, yucca plants, and symbiosis point to a young Creation—a Creation that took place thousands of years ago and not millions or billions? Think about it: if yucca moths need yucca plants to survive, and yucca plants need yucca moths, then both would need to have been created at virtually the same time. The Bible indicates that God made all plant and animal life within three days of each other during the Creation week (Genesis 1:9-25; Exodus 20:11). On the other hand, evolution says that everything evolved gradually over many millions of years. Yet, how could the yucca plant, which needs help pollinating, and the yucca moth, which needs the yucca plant for survival, have been separated by millions of years and still survive? They couldn't. In truth, they were created in the same week only a few thousand years ago— just as the Bible teaches.

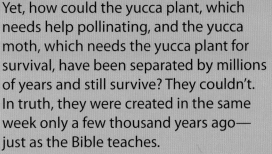

? HAVE YOU CONSIDERED....?

HEAVEN-MADE HONEYBEES AND SWEET SYM-BEE-O-SIS

One of the most important symbiotic relationships on Earth is between honeybees and various forms of vegetation. God made many kinds of fruit trees and plants that need to be pollinated in order for them to bear fruit. How could pollen get transferred from plant to plant, thus fertilizing vegetation and making the growth of fruit, vegetables, and flowers possible? God made flying insects.

It is estimated that nearly one-third of the American diet comes from fruit trees and plants pollinated by insects. Amazingly, about 80% of this vegetation is pollinated specifically by honeybees. Needless to say, bees are important to many kinds of vegetation (and thus to us as well, since we eat fruits and vegetables).

Honeybees, however, also benefit from plants. Honeybees use the pollen from plants as a source of protein, especially for their young. Honeybees also use the nectar from flowers to make honey. So, honeybees help plants, and plants benefit honeybees—a perfect example of symbiosis. The sweet symbiotic relationship between honeybees and vegetation is just another cool confirmation of Creation.

Spiders and their Silk
Show Design

ALTHOUGH SPIDERS GIVE MOST PEOPLE
THE CREEPS, THESE LITTLE CREATURES BEAR WITNESS TO THEIR WONDERFUL CREATOR. TECHNICALLY SPIDERS, AS EIGHT-LEGGED, FANGED
creatures, are classified as arachnids. Generally, however, most people refer to them, along with many other small, invertebrates (backboneless animals), as bugs or insects.

Spiders can be as small as the head of a pin or as large as a dinner plate. They all produce venom, but relatively few are harmful to humans. Spiders, in fact, are very helpful to humans in so far as they eat the insects that often infest houses or damage crops. In recent years, scientists have come to appreciate spiders even more for their super strong silk webbing.

THE GOLIATH BIRDEATER TARANTULA IS THE LARGEST SPIDER IN THE WORLD.

Super-Strong Spider Silk

To the average person, a spider's web looks very weak and flimsy. With the greatest of ease, a person can destroy a web. Even Job's uninspired friend, Bildad, testified to the weakness of webs when he compared the unrighteous to those "whose trust is a spider's web" (Job 8:14), who are leaning upon a house that easily perishes. So why are scientists so awestruck by the spider's silk webbing?

Scientists are fascinated with spider silk because it has the amazing capacity to absorb a strong impact. Think about it. Spider silk is much, much smaller and lighter than the flies and grasshoppers that often fly full speed into a spider's web. Yet the web doesn't break. It stretches but it doesn't break—at least not usually. Spider silk can stretch 30% farther than the stretchiest known nylon and 40% beyond its original length without breaking. Some spiders' webs are so strong, in fact, that they can even catch small birds, such as hummingbirds. (Yes, some spiders will even catch and eat birds.) Although it may not seem strong and tough from the vantage point of a human who easily can tear down a spider's web, pound-for-pound, the silk from certain kinds of spiders is five times stronger than steel, and is twice as strong as the material that currently makes up bulletproof vests. Due to its amazing strength and stretchiness, it has been said that you could trap a jumbo jet with spider silk that is the thickness of a pencil.

SPIDERS TO AVOID INCLUDE THE BROWN RECLUSE AND THE BLACK WIDOW.

Did You Know?

Spider silk is made up of chains of amino acids (protein)—an arrangement that is responsible for the silk's amazing strength. Can you imagine how useful it would be if we could produce our own spider silk? Since harvesting silk from spiders is not very practical, scientists are attempting to make artificial "spider silk" that could be used for countless things, including bridge cables, airbags, and artificial tendons. We could make soft, lightweight, bulletproof vests for policemen—vests that would absorb twice the impact of current ones.

How have scientists fared so far? Although they have made some progress, one scientist admitted that despite years of research, artificial webbing "can't even come close" to equaling the amazing qualities of spider-produced silk. Sadly, this same scientist believes that spiders just "evolved the capacity to spin silk." Are we to believe that the mastermind behind the light, stretchy, shock-absorbing, tougher-than-steel, better-than-anything-man-made, spider webbing is mindless evolution? Absurd!

Obviously, if scientists must spend countless hours trying to design a way to reproduce spider silk, it makes no sense to believe that the natural silk, which spiders make, is a product of mutations, time, chance, and non-intelligence. Spider webbing is God's wonder material. That is, God designed these arachnids with the amazing ability to weave wonderful webs. Truly, "the foolishness of God is wiser than men, and the weakness of God is stronger than men" (1 Corinthians 1:25).

Conclusion

EVOLUTION or CREATION?

ACCORDING TO

THE GENERAL THEORY OF EVOLUTION, ABOUT 13-14 BILLION YEARS AGO ALL OF the matter in the Universe was located in one very dense little spot, smaller than the period at the end of this sentence. As the story goes, this spot exploded, which allegedly resulted in the formation of millions of galaxies, including the Milky Way Galaxy in which we live. Billions of years later, the Earth came to be in its present form. Then, over millions of years, something non-living somehow turned into something living. Eventually, after many millions of years of mindless, aimless evolution, the Earth became filled with a variety of amazing, wonderfully designed animals.

Every life form that allegedly evolved on Earth is said to have come about by unintelligent, random chance over millions of years. Some life forms "just happened" to evolve the ability to breathe oxygen, while others "just happened" to develop the capability to live in the seas and extract oxygen from water. Some life forms "just happened" to evolve the ability to walk up and down vertical ledges (geckos), while others "just happened" to evolve the ability to fly

Green Lynx Spider

COMPLEX deSign (like that FOUND throughout the ANIMAL Kingdom) deMANds AN INtelligent DeSigner.

thousands of miles through the air (bar-tailed godwits). Some life forms "just happened" to evolve the ability to make silk (spiders), while others "just happened" to evolve the "gift" of glowing (lightning bugs). Allegedly, every animal on Earth has come into existence by random, chance happenings over billions of years. According to the General Theory of Evolution, there was no mind, no intelligence, and no designer that created the Universe and everything in it.

Reason, common sense, and true science demand a better explanation. The Law of Cause and Effect says that all physical effects must have **adequate** causes that come before or are simultaneous with their effects. Are random chances and mindlessness great enough causes to bring about the navigation system of a bar-tailed godwit or the camouflage abilities of a cuttlefish? Complex design (like that found throughout the Animal Kingdom) demands an intelligent Designer. A painting demands a painter, a poem a poet, a law a lawgiver, and a plan a planner. The amazing, well-designed animals all around us demand a Creator.

On May 24, 1844, Samuel Morse, who invented the telegraph system and Morse Code, sent the very first telegraph from Washington, D.C. to Baltimore, Maryland. This message consisted of a brief quotation from Numbers 23:23 (KJV): "What hath **God wrought!**" Samuel Morse boldly testified to what everyone should understand: design demands a designer. Morse's code and the telegraph system were the immediate effects of a designer: Samuel Morse. But, the Grand Designer is God, Who created Morse and every material thing that Morse used to invent his telegraph system. Samuel Morse recognized this marvelous, self-evident truth. Should we not recognize it as well, especially in view of the amazing animals that inhabit planet Earth?

The General Theory of Evolution tells man to look to nature and learn from what **evolution has worked.** Yet, nature actually testifies loudly to what "**God has worked!**" In reality, "the whole earth is full of **His** glory" (Isaiah 6:3). "**He** who built all things is **God**" (Hebrews 3:4).

*"Since the creation of the world His invisible attributes are clearly seen, being understood **by the things that are made**, even His [God's] eternal power and Godhead"* (Romans 1:20).

*"This great and wide sea, in which are innumerable teeming things, living things both small and great. O Lord, how manifold are Your works! In wisdom **You have made them all**"* (Psalm 104:25,24).

WORKS CONSULTED

Web Sites

American Museum of National History (amnh.org)
AnswersinGenesis.org
ApologeticsPress.org
AustralianFauna.com
Britannica.com
BusinessWeek.com
Creation.com
DefenseReview.com
LiveScience.com
NationalGeographic.com
National Wildlife Federation (nwf.org)
Nature.ca
ScienceDaily.com
ScienceNews.org
TechnologyReview.com
Time.com
Wired.com

Books, Magazines, Etc.

The Amazing Story of Creation by Duane Gish
Creation Magazine (Published by Creation Ministries)
Discovery Magazine (Published by Apologetics Press)
Nature Fact File (Published by Grolier, Inc.)
The New Encyclopedia Britannica (1997)
Truth Be Told by Kyle Butt and Eric Lyons
Wildlife Fact File (Published by International Masters)
World Book Encyclopedia (1996)